Lonely planet

POCKET

GLASGOW

TOP EXPERIENCES • LOCAL LIFE

T0021277

ANDY SYMINGTON

Contents

Plan Your Trip   4

Tolbooth Steeple, Glasgow Cross (p90)
SKULLY/SHUTTERSTOCK ©

COVID-19

We have re-checked every business in this book before publication to ensure that it is still open after the COVID-19 outbreak. However, the economic and social impacts of COVID-19 will continue to be felt long after the outbreak has been contained, and many businesses, services and events referenced in this guide may experience ongoing restrictions. Some may be temporarily closed, have changed their opening hours and services, or require bookings; some unfortunately could have closed permanently. We suggest you check with venues before visiting for the latest information.

Glasgow's Top Experiences

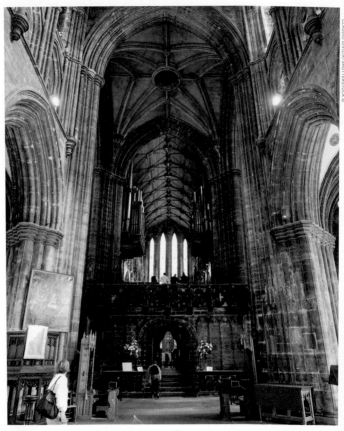

CLAUDIO DIVIZIA/SHUTTERSTOCK ©

Travel Back in Time at Glasgow Cathedral (p60)

**Ponder Big Issues at St Mungo's
Museum of Religious Life & Art (p64)**

BUTTONS AND FLUFFY/SHUTTERSTOCK ©

**Walk Through the Corridors
of Power at City Chambers (p78)**

Watch a Show at Sharmanka Kinetic Theatre (p82)

Hear an Organ Recital at Kelvingrove Art Gallery & Museum (p116)

S-F/SHUTTERSTOCK ©

EQROY/SHUTTERSTOCK © ARCHITECTS: BDP

Get Interactive at Glasgow Science Centre (p104)

Explore a Tall Ship at Riverside Museum (p102)

JEWHYTE/GETTY IMAGES © ARCHITECTS: ZAHA HADID

ANDREYSPB2I/SHUTTERSTOCK ©

Marvel at the Victorian University of Glasgow (p120)

Dining Out

Glasgow is the best place to eat in Scotland, with a stupendous range of restaurants and cafes. The West End is a culinary centre, with Merchant City also boasting a high concentration of quality establishments. Pubs and bars are often good mealtime options too.

Dining Scene

Glasgow's eating scene is Scotland's best and is delightfully informal; even the city's top restaurants have zero airs and graces. Though you can still chow down on a deep-fried Mars bar or a Clydeside Heartstopper, the city has long since diversified from that dubious legacy. West End options like the long-time pioneer Ubiquitous Chip (p134) have set a standard for quality Scottish produce elaborated with multicultural influences, gimmick-free innovation and casual sophistication that is now being reproduced and riffed on all over town. The city's legendary curry houses offer another delicious option.

Eating Zones

In many ways, the West End is the powerhouse of Glasgow's foodie scene, with the area around Byres Rd a hub of quality eating and Argyle St in Finnieston a heartland of fashionable new eating options. Great Western Rd and Gibson St also offer excellent choices.

A plethora of cafes, pubs and restaurants of all origins makes Merchant City another of the city's key dining destinations. There's enough here at lunchtime to entice you, but it's in the evening that the place really comes into its own.

Best Modern Scottish

Ubiquitous Chip Still the flagship of Glasgow's quality dining scene. (p134)

Stravaigin Always experimenting with solid Scottish produce. (p130)

Gannet A standout in the fashionable Finnieston strip. (p135)

RAVID_COHEN/SHUTTERSTOCK ©

Cail Bruich This unassuming West End spot offers great produce and presentation. (p134)

Gamba Basement restaurant showcasing top Scottish seafood. (p49)

Best Vegetarian

Saramago Café Bar In an arts centre, with great atrium eating and an upstairs bar. (p44)

Hug & Pint Innovative vegan food drawing on exotic flavours. (p138)

Mono Browse the record store while you wait for your veggie comfort food. (p91)

Picnic Likeable Merchant City vegan lunch stop. (p91)

Best South Asian

Mother India She's mothered Glasgow with delicious curries for years. (p131; pictured)

Ranjit's Kitchen Ranjit and family turn out quality Punjabi specialities. (p111)

Dakhin Light, flavoursome, gluten-free South Indian curry. (p93)

Wee Curry Shop Squeeze in for lunch. (p44)

Best Seafood

Gamba Fine fish in this sizeable below-street-level restaurant. (p49)

The Finnieston Sip a quality G&T before tucking into sustainable fish. (p132)

Top Tips for Eating Out 🍽️

○ The excellent *Eating & Drinking Guide*, published by *The List* every second April, covers both Glasgow and Edinburgh.

○ Many Glasgow restaurants post offers online (changing daily) at www.5pm.co.uk.

Bar Open

Glaswegians are known to enjoy a beverage or two, and some of Britain's best nightlife is found in the din and sometimes roar of the city's pubs and bars. There are as many different styles of bar as there are punters to guzzle in them. Craft beer, single malt, Scottish gins; it's all here.

The Scene

Glaswegians definitely work to live, and the city comes into its own after five – not that people don't pop down for a cheeky lunchtime pint, too. The city's pubs are gloriously friendly places and you're sure to have some entertaining *blethers* (chats) with locals when you pop into one. Glasgow's live music scene is also legendary; big bands play at iconic venues, but a number of lower-key pubs have regular gigs that are excellent too. Clubbing is also popular, with a couple of famous dance floors, and the LGBT-focused Pink Triangle is a notably friendly scene.

Pub Culture

The local pub is still the staple hub of social life in Glasgow; traditional venues like The Pot Still (p50) take their place alongside stylish city-centre bars and quite a few spots focused on craft beer. Apart from having a drink, pubs are places to read the paper, to meet friends, to make new ones, to watch the *fitba* (football), to have a meal, to flirt and to relax. Even if drinking isn't your thing, it's still worth trying out a few pubs; you're likely to find the soul of Glasgow there.

Best Beer

Drygate Watch the factory floor while you sip a pint. (p71)

DogHouse Merchant City Start trying the range. (p94)

Shilling Brewing Co Some lovely craft beers in an old bank. (p50)

West on the Green German-style beer hall with its own brews. (p72)

PAWEL KMIEC/ALAMY STOCK PHOTO ©

Innis & Gunn Beer Kitchen Plenty of taps on Ashton Lane. (p137)

Best Outdoor Drinking

Inn Deep Marvellous atmosphere by the River Kelvin. (p135)

Brel The tiered terrace here is a magical spot to be. (p136)

West on the Green Sit out and overlook Glasgow Green. (p72)

The Finnieston Grab a pew in the little gin garden out the back. (p132)

Babbity Bowster Outdoor tables to watch Merchant City life go by. (p95)

Best Clubs

Sub Club Long been legendary but still a cracking nightclub. (p49)

Polo Lounge Show your moves in the heart of the Pink Triangle. (p96)

Classic Grand Lots of fun when they crank up the powerpop. (p52)

Buff Club Attitude-free place for relaxed clubbing. (p50)

Nice 'n' Sleazy The weekend club here is wildly popular with a young crowd. (p52)

Best Cocktails & Spirits

Kelvingrove Café Excellent cocktails in this moody Finnieston locale. (p136)

The Finnieston Take the bartender's advice and try an offbeat G&T combination. (p132)

Bar Gandolfi Refined upstairs spot for a quiet martini. (p94)

The Pot Still Venerable pub with a fabulous single malt selection. (p50)

Tiki Bar Get into the swing with something a little Pacific. (p51)

Rum Shack Set sail for the Spanish Main or at least to the Southside. (p112)

Treasure Hunt

Glasgow is where Scotland shops; the city packs out at weekends when highlanders, islanders, Edinburghers and more come in to cruise the malls. The downtown area has several major shopping centres and arcades. On the fringes and in the West End are the bohemian beats: record stores, vintage clothing markets and more.

The Shopping Scene

The 'Style Mile' around Buchanan St, Argyle St and Merchant City (particularly upmarket Ingram St) is a fashion hub, while the West End has quirkier, more bohemian options and is great for vintage clothing. In the East End, the weekend Barras market is quite an experience, blending modern concepts with cheap designer ripoffs, faded bric-a-brac and a dose of authentic working-class Glasgow.

Vintage Shopping

Glasgow has an excellent collection of vintage shops and markets that make finding preloved denim or the perfect piece of nostalgia to sit on top of the TV (remember that?) a piece of cake. The West End has a rich seam to mine, where the area's high student population keenly browse the second-hand clothing, books and music from a wide selection of shops. Near the city centre, Mr Ben (p97) is a standout for 1970s and '80s fashion, while

Barras market is another treasure trove.

Best Shopping

Mr Ben From Fred Perry to ski jackets, it's here. (p97)

Argyll Arcade Fabulous traditional jewellery arcade. (p98)

Randall's Antique & Vintage Centre Astonishing array of blasts from the past. (p75)

Barras Art & Design This art and design hub is rejuvenating the Barras weekend market. (p73)

Best Vintage

Mr Ben Lots of classic vintage clothing labels. (p97)

Randall's Antique & Vintage Centre Huge selec-

CORNFIELD/SHUTTERSTOCK ©

tion of stalls selling vintage curios. (p75)

Glasgow Vintage Company Small but quality selection of preloved clothes. (p138)

Antiques & Interiors Retro delights up the end of Ruthven Lane. (p141)

Best Markets

The Barras Glasgow's famous weekend market is highly entertaining. (p73)

Super Market Wide selection of stalls in an atmospheric space. (p56)

Merchant Square Craft & Design Fair Stalls selling handmade crafts in this covered venue. (p99)

Best Food & Drink

Valhalla's Goat Striking name, striking wine, beer and chocolate selection. (p139)

George Mewes Cheese Fabulous Byres Rd cheese shop. (p139)

Roots, Fruits and Flowers A wide selection of quality vegetarian produce. (p139)

Inverarity One to One Excellent Bath St wine dealer. (p56)

Best Clothing

Slanj Kilts One of the best places to pick up some tartan. (p56)

Princes Square Several notable upmarket boutiques. (p98)

Buchanan Galleries Huge selection of clothing stores. (p57; pictured)

Celtic Shop Get your green and white hoops here. (p56)

Show Time

Glasgow is Scotland's entertainment city, from classical music, fine theatres and ballet to an amazing range of live music venues. To tap into the scene, check out The List (www.list.co.uk), an invaluable free events guide. For theatre tickets, book directly with the venues. For concerts, a useful booking centre is Tickets Scotland.

Live Music

Glasgow is the king of Scotland's live music scene. Year after year, touring musicians and travellers alike name Glasgow one of their favourite cities in the world to enjoy live music. Much of Glasgow's character is encapsulated in the soul and humour of its inhabitants, and the main reason for the city's musical success lies within its audience and the musical community it has bred and nurtured for years.

There are so many venues it's impossible to keep track of them all. For the latest listings, pick up a copy of the *Gig Guide* or check its website (www. gigguide.co.uk). It's available free in most pubs and venues.

Football

Two football clubs – Rangers and Celtic – totally dominate the sporting scene in Scotland (p74).

Best Entertainment

King Tut's Wah Wah Hut Famous venue with nightly bands. (p54; pictured)

Celtic FC Catch the Hoops playing in green and white at home. (p72)

Rangers FC If blue is your colour, head to a game at Ibrox. (p112)

Glasgow Film Theatre Excellent art-house cinema. (p54)

Tramway There's always something interesting on at this vibrant Southside spot. (p112)

Hug and Pint Super-cordial pub for live music and meat-free grub. (p138)

Best Live Music

King Tut's Wah Wah Hut This unassuming-looking basement is an iconic British venue. (p54; pictured)

Hydro Lures some of music's biggest names to Glasgow. (p112)

Barrowland Ballroom The down-at-heel glamour

SLIDEWARRIOR/SHUTTERSTOCK ©

gives this dancehall unique atmosphere. (p73)

13th Note Café Vegetarian cafe with regular live music downstairs. (p97)

Glasgow Royal Concert Hall Home of the Royal Scottish National Orchestra. (p55)

Nice 'n' Sleazy Famous student dive bar with regular gigs. (p52)

Hug and Pint Charming venue at the beginning of the West End for music and vegan food. (p138)

St Luke's & the Winged Ox Lots of bands in this converted church. (p72)

MacSorley's Something is on each night of the week at this handsome old boozer. (p51)

Best Classical Music

Glasgow Royal Concert Hall, classical concerts and more. (p55)

Theatre Royal The city's principal opera venue. (p55)

City Halls Catch the Scottish Symphony here. (p97)

Best Theatres & Performance Spaces

Citizens' Theatre One of Scotland's premier theatres. (p112)

Tramway Avant-garde community hub. (p112)

Centre for Contemporary Arts Eclectic offering of all types of performance. (p55)

A Play, A Pie and a Pint Lunchtime shows in the pub. (p138)

Best Concert Venues

Barrowland Ballroom This creaky old charmer is still super atmospheric. (p73)

Hydro Space-age design and acoustics. (p112)

Glasgow Academy This Southside former cinema hosts big-name bands. (p113)

Active Glasgow

Glasgow's weather means that it's not a city with myriad options for outdoor pursuits, but there are some good choices. There's a wide range of walking trails in and around the city, as well as walking and cycling tours available. Powerboats and an old paddle steamer can get you out on the Clyde.

Walking & Cycling

There are numerous green spaces within the city. Pollok Country Park surrounds the Burrell Collection (p108) and has several woodland trails. Nearer the centre of the city, the **Kelvin Walkway** follows the River Kelvin through Kelvingrove Park (p128), the Botanic Gardens and on to Dawsholm Park.

The Clyde Walkway (p108) stretches from Glasgow upriver to the Falls of Clyde near New Lanark, about 40 miles away. The tourist office (p148) has information outlining different sections of this walk. The 10-mile section through Glasgow has interesting parts, though most of the old shipyards are no longer there. There are some beautiful sections further upstream.

The well-trodden, long-distance footpath the **West Highland Way** begins in Milngavie, 8 miles north of Glasgow (you can walk to Milngavie from Glasgow along the River Kelvin), and runs for 95 spectacular miles to Fort William.

There are several long-distance pedestrian/cycle routes that begin in Glasgow and follow off-road routes for most of the way. Check www.sustrans.org.uk for more details.

The **Clyde–Loch Lomond route** traverses residential and industrial areas in a 20-mile ride from Bell's Bridge to Loch Lomond. This route continues to Inverness, part of the **Lochs and Glens National Cycle Route**.

DAVID MCELROY/SHUTTERSTOCK ©

The **Clyde to Forth cycle route** runs through Glasgow. One way takes you to Edinburgh via Bathgate, the other takes you via Paisley to Greenock and Gourock, the first section partly on roads. Another branch heads down to Irvine and Ardrossan, for the ferry to Arran. An extension via Ayr, Maybole and Glentrool leads to the Solway coast and Carlisle.

Best Walking Spots

Clyde Walkway Tackle a section of this 40-mile path. (p108)

Botanic Gardens These lovely gardens are a major attraction in the West End. (p128; pictured)

Fossil Grove See this petrified forest, then explore the living park. (p128)

Burrell Collection Part of this gallery's appeal is the glorious parkland around it. (p108)

Glasgow Green By the Clyde, this is the city's oldest park. (p70)

Glasgow Necropolis Part park, part cemetery, all intriguing. (p63)

Kelvingrove Park Greenery and a pretty river by the university in the West End. (p128)

Queens Park Attractive Southside park with duck pond and views. (p110)

Architecture & Design

The work of Charles Rennie Mackintosh gives Glasgow an instant appeal for lovers of architecture and design, with his buildings and creations spread across the city. Newer masterpieces turn heads, while the Victorian grandeur of the city centre provides a dignified background.

Glasgow Architecture

Glasgow's principal architectural legacy is its impressive assemblage of stately Victorian mansions and public buildings, the product of wealth generated from manufacturing and trade. It gives the centre a solid, slightly staid dignity that is actually rather misleading. More svelte are the sublime designs of Charles Rennie Mackintosh that dot the city; visiting a few of his buildings and interiors soon reveals his genius. The city – always proud of its working-class background – also innovatively displays its industrial heritage, while modern structures, many along the Clyde River, have quickly become local icons.

Best Charles Rennie Mackintosh

Mackintosh House Sumptuous interior of the Mackintoshes' first conjugal home. (p121)

Mackintosh at the Willow Reconstruction of his classic design of a venue for cakes and a cuppa. (p42)

The Lighthouse Tucked away in the centre, this has a detailed design exhibition. (p42)

Mackintosh Queen's Cross A striking church and HQ of the Mackintosh Society, north of the city centre. (p46)

House for an Art Lover Built posthumously to a Mackintosh design. (p109)

Scotland Street School Museum CRM turned his hand to education at this Southside primary school. (p108)

EQROY/SHUTTERSTOCK ©

Glasgow School of Art His supreme creation, tragically fire-damaged but to be rebuilt. (p42)

Kelvingrove Art Gallery & Museum Good background information on the architect and his wife. (p116)

Daily Record Building This former newspaper headquarters is rather underwhelmingly set on a narrow lane. (p43)

Best Modern Architecture

Riverside Museum The late Zaha Hadid designed this shimmering transport museum. (p102; pictured)

Hydro This 'take me to your leader' mothership is a striking sight. (p112)

Clyde Auditorium The much-loved 'armadillo' still turns heads. (p112)

Glasgow School of Art Opposite the damaged Mackintosh masterpiece is the cool, crisp, contemporary Reid Building. (p42)

Worth a Trip: Hill House

In Helensburgh, northwest of Glasgow on the Clyde estuary, **Hill House** (p45) is perhaps Charles Rennie Mackintosh's finest creation – its timeless elegance still feels chic today. The interiors are stunning, with rose motifs and fabulous furniture. Water soaking through the rendered cement exterior means that you'll find the house enclosed in a giant covering structure. The house also has a beautiful garden.

Tours

Compared to other cities of its size, Glasgow doesn't have a huge range of tours, but there are certainly options. Walking and cycling tours examine some of the city's lesser-known sights, including one that takes you behind the scenes at Glasgow Central station. The standard hop-on-hop-off bus circuit is also available.

COMPLEXLI/SHUTTERSTOCK ©

Glasgow Central Tours (www.glasgowcentraltours.co.uk; tour £13; ⊙check website for tour times) A passionate guide takes you around and under Glasgow Central station. Hidden spaces, an abandoned Victorian platform and lots of information make this a fascinating experience. It lasts about an hour; check the website for dates. The minimum age is 12 years.

Glasgow Bike Tours (☏0141-374 2342; www.glasgowbiketours.co.uk; 28 Vinicombe St; adult/child £30/15) A friendly guide runs a three-hour circuit around the city. It takes in several key sights around the periphery of the city centre and gets you an especially good look at the Clyde and the West End.

Waverley (☏0141-221 8152; www.waverleyexcursions.co.uk; ⊙mid-May–mid-Aug plus some Oct departures) The world's last ocean-going paddle steamer (built in 1947; pictured) cruises Scotland's west coast in summer, with many different routes; the website details days of departure. Its Glasgow departures are from the Glasgow Science Centre.

Seaforce (☏0141-221 1070; www.seaforce.co.uk; Riverside Museum) Departing from the Riverside Museum, Seaforce offers speedy powerboat jaunts along the Clyde. Trips include a 20-minute 'Clyde Ride' around central Glasgow (adult/child £10/5). They run year-round but call ahead as they are weather dependent.

Glasgow Taxis City Tour (☏0141-429 7070; www.glasgowtaxis.co.uk) A 60-minute taxi tour is a good way to get a feel of the city and its sights. The standard tour costs £35 for up to five people, or £65 for two hours.

City Sightseeing (☏0141-204 0444; www.citysightseeingglasgow.co.uk; adult/child £16/9; ⊙9.30am-4.30pm) These hop-on-hop-off, double-decker tourist buses run a sightseeing circuit, starting on George Sq. Departures every 15 minutes (30 minutes from November to March). A ticket bought from the driver, online (£1 cheaper) or in the tourist office, is valid for one or two days. All buses have wheelchair access and multilingual commentary.

ESSEVU/SHUTTERSTOCK ©

Under the Radar

You could say Glasgow as a whole has traditionally slipped under the radar, its many charms far less widely trumpeted than Edinburgh's. And it's all the better for it. Going under the radar in Glasgow means exploring its lifestyle and countercultures, getting the feel of the differences between its varied neighbourhoods and – crucially – chatting to as many locals as possible.

Off the Beaten Track

Within striking distance of the city centre are plenty of neighbourhoods where most visitors barely scratch the surface. Often it just takes walking a street or two beyond – push into Glasgow's east end beyond the cathedral; explore the west away from Byres Road; and get to know Southside's increasingly trendy hubs. Glasgow's easy-to-navigate circular subway line is particularly helpful for exploring the west and the south.

Down with the Locals

Surely one of the most gregarious cities going,

Glasgow rewards the visitor who gets blethering (chatting) with the locals, your surefire pathway to an authentic urban experience. Some places to meet them:

Gigs Glasgow's live music scene is a great way to feel the pulse of the city. There are bands on every night, from big names on UK tours to young musos rocking a local pub.

Parks Local parks such as Glasgow Green (p70; pictured) or Queens Park (p110) are hubs of local life, where you'll find Glaswegians strolling, canoodling, gushing over pretty pooches and bonnie babies or stripping down to sunbathe whenever the temperature threatens to get above 15°C.

Football Celtic (p72) and Rangers (p112) FCs are the big-ticket teams in town, but for a more under-the-radar experience head to Firhill Stadium (in Maryhill) to watch Partick Thistle, or watch a Queens Park game: they may play in Scotland's national stadium, Hampden Park, but you could probably meet everyone in the crowd by the time the 90 minutes is up.

Pubs The West End, Bath Street and Merchant City are full of casually stylish places to drink and are top spots to meet young Glaswegians. But don't miss out on some of the more traditional drinking dens...hearing an old-timer tell tales of the city over a pint is a quintessential Glasgow experience.

Festivals & Events

SKULLY/SHUTTERSTOCK ©

Celtic Connections
(☎0141-353 8000; www.celticconnections.com; ⊙Jan) This two-week music festival focuses on roots music and folk from Scotland and around the world.

Glasgow Film Festival
(www.glasgowfilm.org; ⊙Feb) Two-week film festival with screenings in various locations across the city.

Glasgow International Comedy Festival
(☎0844 873 7353; www.glasgowcomedyfestival.com; ⊙Mar) Two weeks of quality comedy, both home-grown and imported, enlivens stages across the city in March.

Glasgow International
(☎0141-276 8384; www.glasgowinternational.org; ⊙late Apr) Held in even-numbered years, this festival features a range of innovative installations, performances and exhibitions around town.

Southside Fringe
(www.southsidefringe.org.uk; ⊙May) This increasingly popular festival focuses on the suburbs south of the Clyde with two weeks of performances in various venues.

West End Festival
(☎0141-341 0844; www.westendfestival.co.uk; ⊙Jun) This music and arts event (pictured above left) is Glasgow's biggest festival. Runs for three weeks.

Glasgow Jazz Festival
(www.jazzfest.co.uk; ⊙Jun) Excellent festival sees big-name international acts come to town, with stages set up in George Sq and Merchant City.

TRNSMT
(www.trnsmtfest.com) Held over two consecutive weekends in late June and early July, this festival only started in 2017 but has been a huge success, drawing major indie rock acts to Glasgow Green.

Merchant City Festival
(www.merchantcityfestival.com; ⊙late Jul) Lively week-long street festival in the Merchant City quarter, with lots of performances and stalls.

World Pipe Band Championships
(www.theworlds.co.uk; ⊙mid-Aug) Held on Glasgow Green, this two-day bagpipe extravaganza features over 200 pipe bands from a surprising number of nations.

For Kids

Glasgow is easy to visit with children due to its extensive public transport system and friendly locals. The city boasts excellent family attractions and there are several apartment-hotels around town. In general, restaurants are well geared for children, and lots of places to eat serve food throughout the day.

ULMUS MEDIA/SHUTTERSTOCK ©

Need to Know

For suggestions for short-term child-care agencies, contact the council-run **Glasgow Family Information Service** (📞0141-287 4702; www.gfis.org.uk).

Most parks in Glasgow have playgrounds for children.

Major shopping complexes are handy stops, with baby-changing facilities and soft play areas.

In family-licensed pubs, accompanied children under 14 years old are admitted between 11am and 8pm.

Best for Kids

Riverside Museum This museum of transport has a tall ship, trains, steamrollers, fire engines and more. (p102)

Glasgow Science Centre A world of discovery for all ages that could occupy several hours. (p104)

Sharmanka Kinetic Theatre Enter a realm of strange and wonderful creations at this curious place. (p82)

Kelvingrove Art Gallery & Museum Entertaining natural history displays and art with informative panels aimed at kids at this excellent museum. (p116; pictured above right)

Scottish Football Museum Learn about the limited glory days of the Scottish national team or take a stadium tour. Celtic and Rangers also offer tours of their sizeable grounds. (p109)

People's Palace Child-friendly displays on the city's history at this museum on Glasgow Green. (p69)

Scotland Street School Museum See how other eras did schooling at this Mackintosh building. (p108)

LGBTIQ+

Glasgow's approachability and friendliness extends to its LGBTIQ+ scene, which is focused on a handful of streets in the Merchant City area. Known as the Pink Triangle, the main zone includes pubs, bars, clubs and shops, with a low-key daytime vibe morphing into happy party nights with a lot less attitude (bouncers apart) than is the norm.

MONICA WELLS/ALAMY STOCK PHOTO ©

Where to Go

Many straight clubs and bars have gay and lesbian nights. To tap into the scene, check out *The List* (www.list.co.uk) and the free *Scots Gay* (www.scotsgay.co.uk) magazine and website. Go early to pick up discounted club admission from one of the drinking venues.

Tolerance

Most Glaswegians are very tolerant, but you may encounter disapproval away from central areas. Same-sex marriage was legalised in Scotland in 2014.

Best LGBTIQ+ Venues

Speakeasy Great atmosphere at this casual bar-diner. (p95)

Waterloo Bar Old favourite with a non-sceney pub atmosphere. (p52)

Katie's Bar Popular with women, this is a friendly pre-clubber. (p95; pictured above left)

AXM Lots of fun at this late-night club. (p96)

Underground Indie basement venue in the heart of the Pink Triangle. (p96)

Delmonica's Well-established pub for pre-club drinks. (p96)

Polo Lounge Beautiful people and a strict door policy at this famous club. (p96)

Museums & Galleries

Collecting was big in Victorian times, so it's no surprise that Glasgow's architectural legacy from the period is complemented by some wonderful museums and galleries.

CORNFIELD/SHUTTERSTOCK ©

Best Galleries

Kelvingrove Art Gallery & Museum Glasgow's museum flagship has an excellent art collection. (p116)

Burrell Collection In the city's south, this is a superb and eclectic collection. Reopening 2022. (p108)

Hunterian Art Gallery Based at the university, this is strong on the Glasgow Boys and other locals. (p121)

Gallery of Modern Art Great juxtaposition of modern works in a classical 19th-century building. (p90)

Best Museums

Kelvingrove Art Gallery & Museum The old-fashioned collection has been repurposed brilliantly. (p116)

Glasgow Science Centre Massive amounts of fun for all ages at this interactive attraction. (p104)

Riverside Museum Clydeside extravaganza of transport. (p102)

Hunterian Museum Browse this gloriously eclectic university collection. (p121)

People's Palace Discover the social history of the city. (p69)

St Mungo's Museum of Religious Life & Art Excellent museum of comparative religion. (p64)

Museum of Piping Discover the secrets of the bagpipes. (p42)

Tenement House Head back in time in this intriguing house museum. (p43)

Scottish Football Museum Discover the highs and lows of Scottish football. (p109)

Scotland Street School Museum Head back to the classroom in this Mackintosh-designed school. (p108; pictured above right)

Four Perfect Days

Day 1

CLAUDIO DIVIZIA/SHUTTERSTOCK ©

Start by visiting **Glasgow Cathedral** (p60; pictured) and the hillside **necropolis** (p63). Then drop into **St Mungo's Museum** (p64) and nose around **Provand's Lordship** (p69), Glasgow's oldest house. Stroll down to Merchant City for lunch.

Next, saunter around the noble trade-baron buildings such as the **Corinthian Club** (p94) and **Trades Hall** (p90). Then pop in for a session at the gloriously offbeat **Sharmanka Kinetic Theatre** (p82).

In the evening, try the many Merchant City pubs, see a gig at **13th Note Café** (p97), a concert at **City Halls** (p97) or hit **Bar Gandolfi** (p94) for cocktails. This is also the heart of Glasgow's LGBTIQ+ nightlife, with several venues.

Day 2

ATOSAN/SHUTTERSTOCK ©

Perk up with coffee at **Riverhill Coffee Bar** (p44) then stroll the central pedestrian area, popping into handsome **Argyll Arcade** (p98) and **Princes Square** (p98). Meander westward to **Mackintosh at the Willow** (p42).

Post-lunch, head to **Kelvingrove Art Gallery & Museum** (p116; pictured) and spend the afternoon marvelling at the collection. Afterwards, stroll the adjacent parkland or nip across to **Brewdog Glasgow** (p136) for a well-deserved pint.

The Finnieston strip is great for dinner, or you might have tickets for a big-name concert at nearby **Hydro** (p112). Otherwise, check out bands at legendary **King Tut's Wah Wah Hut** (p54).

Day 3

Investigate the fine **Hunterian Art Gallery** (p121), the diverse collection of the **Hunterian Museum** (p121) and the gorgeous interior of **Mackintosh House** (p121), all part of the **University of Glasgow** (p120).

Spend the afternoon roaming Byres Rd, checking out vintage shops and quality delicatessens. Take a lengthy stroll in the **Botanic Gardens** (p128) and check out the pretty River Kelvin, dropping by **Inn Deep** (p135) for a waterside pint.

Dine at legendary **Ubiquitous Chip** (p134; pictured) then see what's going down at the former church **Òran Mór** (p136). Otherwise, walk on and see who's playing at the **Hug & Pint** (p138).

Day 4

Check out the fabulous **Burrell Collection** (p108), due to reopen in 2022. Otherwise, hit the **Riverside Museum** (p102) or check out Mackintosh's **Scotland Street School Museum** (p108) and **House for an Art Lover** (p109).

Investigate Glasgow's social history and the greenhouse at the **People's Palace** (p69; pictured) in the city's oldest park, then head downtown and browse shops along Buchanan St, dropping into **The Lighthouse** (p42) for the view and more Mackintoshiana.

Book at **Gamba** (p49) for quality seafood then head to **Horse Shoe** (p52) or **The Pot Still** (p50) for a traditional pub experience. Afterwards, hit the famous **Sub Club** (p49) for quality DJs.

Need to Know

For detailed information, see Survival Guide (p143).

Population
596,500

Currency
Pound (£)

Language
English

Visas
Generally not needed for stays of up to six months.

Money
ATMs (cashpoints) widely available. Credit cards are accepted in most (but not all) places, sometimes with a minimum spend or surcharge.

Time
Western European Time (GMT/UTC)

Phones
The UK uses the GSM 900/1800 network. Local SIM cards can be used in unlocked phones.

Tipping
10% in restaurants, round up in taxis.

Daily Budget

Budget: Less than £65
Dorm bed: £24–34
Fish supper: £5–8
Museum entry: many are free
Daily bus ticket: £4.50

Midrange: £65–150
Double room at midrange B&B: £70–100
Bar lunch: £10
Dinner for two at midrange restaurant: £60–90
Taxi across town: £6–10

Top end: More than £150
Double room at high-end hotel: £130–250
Dinner for two at high-end restaurant: £100–160
Cocktails: £8–14
Ticket to a show: £20–70

Useful Websites

People Make Glasgow (www.peoplemake glasgow.com) City-run website with events and more.

The List (www.list.co.uk) Comprehensive entertainment listings and restaurant reviews.

Herald Scotland (www.heraldscotland.com) Glasgow's broadsheet, printed since 1783.

Glasgow Food Geek (www.glasgowfoodgeek. co.uk) Likeably unpretentious food blog.

Lonely Planet (www.lonelyplanet.com/scot land/glasgow) Destination information, hotel bookings, traveller forum and more.

SPT (www.spt.co.uk) Glasgow public transport information.

Arriving in Glasgow

✈ Glasgow International Airport

Speedy buses run all day and night to the city centre (25 minutes). A taxi is around £25.

✈ Prestwick Airport

Trains run four times hourly to Glasgow (45 minutes).

✈ Edinburgh Airport

There are direct buses from the airport to Glasgow (one hour).

🚌 Glasgow Central Station

Trains from the south arrive here. It's very central, with good bus connections.

🚌 Buchanan St Bus Station

This is where all intercity bus services terminate; it's a short walk to the centre of town.

⚓ Greenock Cruise Port

Regular trains run from Greenock to Glasgow (35 to 50 minutes).

Getting Around

🚌 Bus

The staple of local transport. Frequent, inexpensive services.

S Subway

Glasgow's underground has just one circular line; it's especially handy for the West End. Finishes early on Sundays.

🚆 Train

Extensive suburban network, useful for reaching some parts of the Southside.

🚲 Bike

Reasonable network of cycle paths, with a cheap and easy citybike scheme.

🚗 Car

Numerous rental companies at airports and downtown. Street parking relatively easy.

Glasgow Neighbourhoods

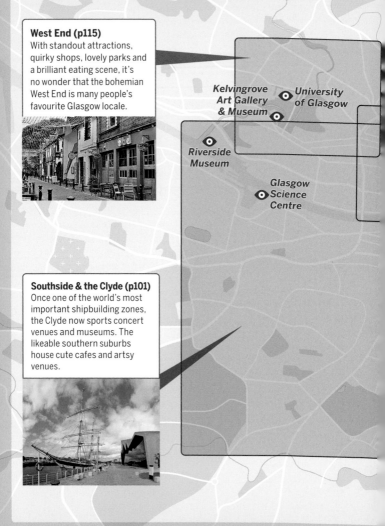

West End (p115)
With standout attractions, quirky shops, lovely parks and a brilliant eating scene, it's no wonder that the bohemian West End is many people's favourite Glasgow locale.

Southside & the Clyde (p101)
Once one of the world's most important shipbuilding zones, the Clyde now sports concert venues and museums. The likeable southern suburbs house cute cafes and artsy venues.

Kelvingrove
Art Gallery
& Museum

University
of Glasgow

Riverside
Museum

Glasgow
Science
Centre

Central Glasgow (p37)
Downtown Glasgow buzzes with urban energy, with a dense eastern half and more spaced-out western streets. Pedestrian shopping strips, bolthole pubs, narrow lanes and elegant terraces comprise its character.

St Mungo's Museum of Religious Life & Art

Glasgow Cathedral

City Chambers

Sharmanka Kinetic Theatre

East End (p59)
The sober beauty of Glasgow's cathedral marks the beginning of this traditionally working class zone, home to the famous Barras markets as well as breweries, craft markets and Celtic FC.

Merchant City (p77)
The stately trade guilds built by the merchant classes make this an area of great architectural dignity, but it's a good-time zone full of restaurants and bars.

Explore
Glasgow

Glasgow's Walking Tours 🚶

Glasgow's West End (p115) GEORGECLERK/GETTY IMAGES ©

Explore ◈
Central Glasgow

Glasgow's centre changes character east to west, going from a frenetic blend of services, transport terminals, pubs and shops to more sedate terraces of thoroughfares like Bath St, where upmarket offices sit over basements converted into stylish bars. Much of the city's quality accommodation clusters here. It's also a student zone, with a nightlife nexus on Sauchiehall St, which runs the length of the neighbourhood.

The grid layout and pedestrian streets of the city centre make it easy to get around, and there are numerous cafes and pubs that make good pit stops between attractions. You may want to mentally divide the downtown area into an eastern and western half. There's more to see in the west – where Mackintosh at the Willow (p42), the damaged Glasgow School of Art (p42) and the nightlife of Bath and Sauchiehall Sts are key drawcards – but the east has more urban energy and life on the street. Quality restaurants and cafes are scattered through the whole area and there are numerous cultural venues.

Getting There & Around

🚌 Glasgow's Buchanan St bus station is located here, and numerous city bus routes traverse the neighbourhood.

🆂 Cowcaddens station is at the northern edge of this region, while St George's Cross station is just to the west of it.

🚆 Both of Glasgow's major train stations are in or by this area.

Central Glasgow Map on p40

Mackintosh at the Willow (p42) STOCKEUROPE/ALAMY STOCK PHOTO ©

Walking Tour 🥾

Art School Life

Glasgow's famous School of Art may be down and damaged but is still iconic. Meanwhile, college life goes on. Around the School are numerous bohemian hang-outs where students and the city's artier souls congregate. If you can't spare the time to enroll in the School, at least you can spend a day pretending that you have.

Walk Facts

Start Renfrew Street;
S Cowcaddens

End Sauchiehall St;
🚃 Numerous

Length 1 mile; 2-3 hours

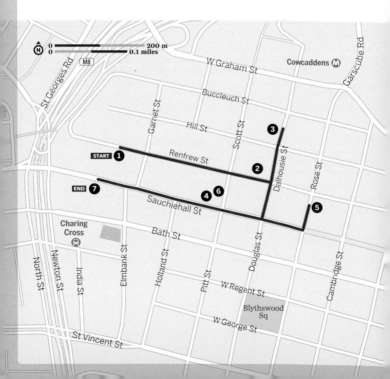

❶ Breakfast in Style

There's something really life-enhancing about the atmosphere at the upbeat basement cafe **Singl-end** (p46). Drop in here for a good cup of coffee and a brunchy meal or sweet snack. Everything is delicious.

❷ The Reid Building

Right opposite the Mackintosh Building, the School of Art's **Reid Building**, designed by Steven Holl, opened in 2014. Its crisp glassy shell contrasted totally with Mackintosh's solid stone, but it worked. Mind you, the School owed us a decent building after the brutalism of the adjacent Bourdon Building that sprawls across Renfrew St like a grey lizard expired from emphysema.

❸ Wash Some Clothes

The laundrette is a student staple and the **Art Laundrette** (p44) is right around the corner from the School of Art. You may not need any clothes washed, but there are exhibitions, workshops and occasional live performances held in this one; poke your nose in to see if anything's on.

❹ Contemporary Art

On Sauchiehall St just below the School of Art, the **Centre for Contemporary Arts** (p55) is just that. It's a hive of creativity; drop by to see what's going down and to check out the visual art exhibition spaces. There are lots of events and performances on here too.

❺ To the Pictures

No serious art student would be seen dead in a mainstream cinema, so it's just as well that the iconic **Glasgow Film Theatre** (p54) is close at hand. Three screens show classic and art-house movies.

❻ On the Deck

Back at the CCA, the vegan food at art-student favourite **Saramago Café Bar** (p44) is pretty delicious. This is also an excellent spot for a drink once the upstairs bar opens at 4pm. Stretch out on the deck on Scott St and watch people struggling up the hill.

❼ Sleazy Does It

There's quite a string of bars on this end of Sauchiehall St and they get quite rowdy later in the evening as young folk lured by cheap lager have a fine old time of it. **Nice 'n' Sleazy** (p52) is one of the best bars here, where students enjoy the wide beer selection, downstairs gigs and late closing.

Central Glasgow

For reviews see

◎ Sights	p42
✕ Eating	p44
⊘ Drinking	p49
✪ Entertainment	p54
⊕ Shopping	p56

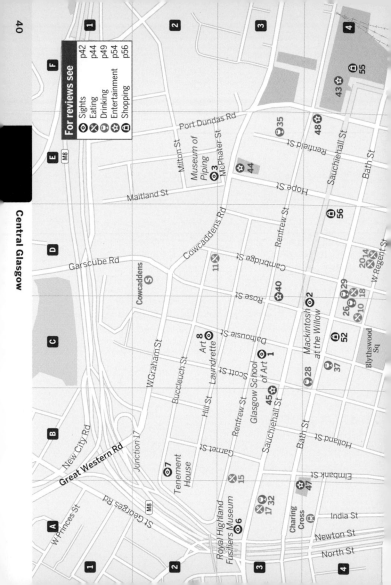

Port Dundas Rd

Museum of Piping ◎3

McPhater St

Maitland St

Milton St

Cowcaddens Rd

Garscube Rd

Cowcaddens Ⓢ

W Graham St

Art ⊕8

Buccleuch St

Laundrette

Dalhousie St

Rose St

Cambridge St

Renfrew St

Hope St

Port Dundas Rd

◎35

44✪

48✪

Renfield St

Sauchiehall St

Bath St

⊕56

Renfrew St

✪40

◎2 Mackintosh at the Willow

26✕ 29

10✕ 18

⊕52

20 14
✕ ⊘
W Regent St

Blythswood Sq

New City Rd

Great Western Rd

St Georges Rd

Junction 17

Tenement House

◎7

Garnet St

Hill St

Scott St

Glasgow School of Art ◎1

45✪

Sauchiehall St

Bath St

Holland St

◎28

37 ⊘

47✪

Charing Cross

Elmbank St

India St

Newton St

North St

Royal Highland Fusiliers Museum ◎6

17 ✕✕ 32

⊘

✕15

43✪

⊕55

Bath St

Sauchiehall St

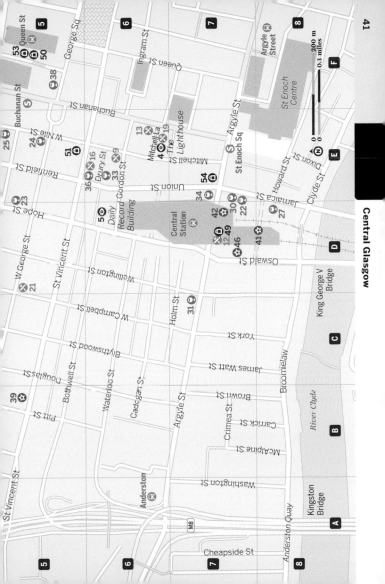

Central Glasgow

Queen St
George Sq
Ingram St
Queen St
53
50
38
Buchanan St
Buchanan St
25
24 W Nile St
51
Renfield St
36 16
Drury St
33 9
Gordon St
Record
Daily
Building
5
23
Hope St
Hope St
W George St
St Vincent St
W George St
21
St Vincent St
Wellington St
W Campbell St
Holm St
31
York St
39
Pitt St
Douglas St
Bothwell St
Waterloo St
Cadogan St
Argyle St
James Watt St
Broomielaw
Crimea St
Carrick St
McAlpine St
Washington St
Anderston
St Vincent St

Argyle
Street
8
St Enoch
Centre
Argyle St
St Enoch Sq
Dixon St
Clyde St
Howard St
Jamaica St
27
22
30
41
46
12 49
42
34
54
Union St
Mitchell St
The
Lighthouse
13
Mitchell La
19
4
Central
Station
Oswald St
King George V
Bridge
River Clyde
Kingston
Bridge
Anderston Quay
Cheapside St
M8

200 m
0.1 miles

F
E
D
C
B
A
5
6
7
8

Sights

Glasgow School of Art

HISTORIC BUILDING

1 ◉ MAP P40, C3

In 2018, Charles Rennie Mackintosh's greatest building was gearing up for reopening after a devastating 2014 fire when, unbelievably, another blaze destroyed the painstakingly reconstructed interiors and severely damaged the building. While the School has committed to reconstructing it, this will be a lengthy process. At time of research the visitor centre, shop and exhibitions in the neighbouring Reid building were closed to visitors; check the website to see if visits and tours have resumed. (📞0141-353 4526; www.gsa.ac.uk; 167 Renfrew St)

Mackintosh at the Willow

HISTORIC BUILDING

2 ◉ MAP P40, C4

Opened in 2018, this reconstruction of the original Willow tearoom that Mackintosh designed and furnished in the early 20th century for restaurateur Kate Cranston offers authentic design splendour in its original location. You can admire the architect's distinctive touch in just about every element; he had free rein and even the teaspoons were given his attention. Alongside the tearoom is a visitor centre, with a two-level interactive exhibition about the historical context and Kate Cranston's collaboration with Mackintosh and Margaret Macdonald. (📞0141-204 1903; www.mackintoshatthewillow.com; 217 Sauchiehall St; exhibition admission adult/child £5.50/3.50; ⏰Opening: Tearoom 9am-5pm, exhibition 9am-5.30pm Mon-Sat, 10am-5pm Sun, last entry 1hr before)

Museum of Piping

MUSEUM

3 ◉ MAP P40, E2

This museum in the national centre for bagpipes covers the history of this Celtic instrument, with several fine historic pieces on display. It's worth coinciding your visit with the guided tours (check online as hours change), which include a demonstration of piping and the chance to have a go yourself. (📞0141-353 0220; www.thepipingcentre.co.uk; 30 McPhater St; adult/child £4.50/2.50; ⏰9am-7pm Mon-Thu, to 5pm Fri, to 3pm Sat)

The Lighthouse

HISTORIC BUILDING

4 ◉ MAP P40, E6

Mackintosh's first building, designed in 1893, was a striking new headquarters for the *Glasgow Herald*. Tucked up a narrow lane off Buchanan St, it now serves as Scotland's Centre for Architecture & Design, with fairly technical temporary exhibitions (sometimes admission is payable for these), as well as the Mackintosh Interpretation Centre, a detailed (if slightly dry) overview of his life and work. On the top floor of the 'lighthouse', drink in great views over the rooftops and spires of the city centre. (📞0141-276 5365; www.thelighthouse.co.uk; 11 Mitchell Lane;

admission free; ⏲10.30am-5pm Mon-Sat, from noon Sun)

Daily Record Building
ARCHITECTURE

5 ◉ MAP P40, D6

This lane seems no showcase for a Charles Rennie Mackintosh building, but here it is. The former headquarters of the *Daily Record* tabloid now contains a popular bar, Stereo. The sandstone pillars, large ground-floor windows and blue- and white-tiled facade deserve a better outlook. (20 Renfield Lane)

Royal Highland Fusiliers Museum
MUSEUM

6 ◉ MAP P40, A3

Charts the history of the Royal Highland Fusiliers, as well as previous regiments, from 1678 to the present. The walls are dripping with exhibits, including uniforms, medals, pictures and other militaria. The wrought iron was designed by Mackintosh. The museum is looking for a new home, so check the website before visiting. (📞0141-332 5639; www.rhf.org.uk; 518 Sauchiehall St; admission free; ⏲9am-4pm Mon-Thu, to 3pm Fri)

Tenement House
HISTORIC BUILDING

7 ◉ MAP P40, B2

For a time-capsule experience, visit this small apartment in a typical tenement building, offering a vivid insight into middle-class city life in the early 20th century (NTS; 📞0141-333 0183; www.nts.org.uk; 145 Buccleuch St; adult/child £7.50/5.50;

The Lighthouse

⏱1-5pm Apr-Jun & Sep-Oct, 11am-5pm Mon-Sat & 1-5pm Sun Jul-Aug)

Art Laundrette

ART STUDIO

8 ◉ MAP P40, C2

This spot around the corner from the School of Art is a laundrette that holds art exhibitions, workshops and events. (📞0141-332 7071; www.facebook.com/The-Art-Laundrette; 39 Dalhousie St; admission free; ⏱9am-6pm Mon-Fri,to 5pm Sat, to 4pm Sun)

Eating

Riverhill Coffee Bar

CAFE $

9 🍴 MAP P40, E6

Chain cafes plaster Glasgow's centre, so it's a joy to come across this tiny place, which offers great coffee and hot chocolate as well as delicious filled rolls and tempting pastries. Ingredients are sustainably sourced and seriously tasty. It's extremely friendly; you'd come every day if you lived nearby. (📞0141-204 4762; www.riverhillcafe. com; 24 Gordon St; rolls £4-5; ⏱7am-5pm Mon-Fri, from 8am Sat, from 10am Sun; 📶)

Saramago Café Bar

CAFE, VEGAN $

In the airy atrium of the Centre for Contemporary Arts (see 45 ✪ Map p40, B3), this place does a great line in eclectic vegan fusion food, with a range of top flavour combinations from around the globe. The upstairs bar (open from 4pm) has a great deck on steep Scott St and packs out inside with a friendly

arty crowd enjoying the DJ sets and quality tap beers. (📞0141-352 4920; www.cca-glasgow.com; 350 Sauchiehall St; mains £8-12; ⏱food noon-10pm Sun-Wed, to 11.30pm Thu-Sat; 📶🍴)

Where the Monkey Sleeps

CAFE $

10 🍴 MAP P40, C4

Laid-back and a bit hippy, this vibrant little number is a perfect escape from the ubiquitous coffee chains. The bagels and panini – with names like Witchfynder or Meathammer – are highlights, as are some very inventive dishes, such as the 'nuclear' beans, dripping with cayenne and Tabasco. (📞0141-226 3406; www.monkey sleeps.com; 182 West Regent St; dishes £3-7; ⏱7am-3pm Mon-Fri; 📶)

Wee Curry Shop

INDIAN $

11 🍴 MAP P40, D2

This tiny place has great home-cooked curries. It's wise to book – it's a snug place with a big reputation, a limited menu and a sensational-value two-course lunch. (📞0141-353 0777; www.wee curryshop.co.uk; 7 Buccleuch St; 2-course lunch £5.95, mains £8-10; ⏱noon-2pm & 5-10.30pm; 📶🍴)

Platform

STREET FOOD $

12 🍴 MAP P40, D7

This atmospheric series of brick-arched vaults under the railway lines at Central station comes into its own at weekends,

Charles Rennie Mackintosh

Great cities have great artists, designers and architects contributing to their urban environment while expressing their soul and individuality. Charles Rennie Mackintosh was all of these and his quirky, linear and geometric designs have had an enormous influence on Glasgow. Many of the buildings Mackintosh designed are open to the public, and you'll see his tall, thin, art-nouveau typeface repeatedly reproduced.

Born in 1868, Mackintosh studied at the Glasgow School of Art. It was there that he met the influential artist and designer Margaret Macdonald, whom he married; they collaborated on many projects and were major influences on each other's work. Together with her sister Frances and Herbert MacNair, the artist who married her, they formed 'The Four', a pioneering group that developed the Glasgow Style. This contribution to art nouveau incorporated influences from the Arts and Crafts movement and Japanese design.

In 1896, aged only 27, Mackintosh won a competition for his design for the new building of the **Glasgow School of Art** (p42), where he had studied. This was his supreme architectural achievement. The first section was opened in 1899 and is considered to be the earliest example of art nouveau in Britain. The second section, opened a decade later, included some of the earliest art deco. The building, under reconstruction again after a second devastating fire in 2018, demonstrates his skill in combining function and style.

Another of Mackintosh's finest works is **Hill House** (☎01436-673900; www.nts.org.uk; Upper Colquhoun St, Helensburgh; adult/child £10.50/7.50; ☉11.30am-5pm Mar-Oct), in Helensburgh. Other buildings around town include the **Daily Record Building** (p43), **Scotland Street School** (p108), **Mackintosh Queen's Cross church** (p46) and **House for an Art Lover** (p109). The reconstructed **MacKintosh at the Willow** (p42) feature his design concepts right down to the smallest level.

Although Mackintosh's genius was quickly recognised in the rest of Europe, he did not receive the same encouragement in Scotland. His architectural career here lasted only until 1914, when he moved to England to concentrate on furniture design. He died in 1928, and it is only since the last decades of the 20th century that Mackintosh's importance has been widely felt. For more about the man and his work, contact the **Charles Rennie Mackintosh Society** (☎0141-946 6600; www.crmsociety.com; Mackintosh Queen's Cross, 870 Garscube Rd). Check its website and www.glasgowmackintosh.com for special events.

Worth a Trip

Now headquarters of the Charles Rennie Mackintosh Society, **Queen's Cross** (☑0141-946 6600; www.mackintoshchurch.com; 870 Garscube Rd; adult/child £4/free; ☻10am-5pm Mon-Fri Apr-Oct, to 4pm Mon, Wed & Fri Nov-Dec & Feb-Mar, closed Jan) is the only one of Mackintosh's church designs to be built. It has an excellent stained-glass window and exquisite relief carvings, and the wonderful simplicity and grace of the barrel-shaped design is particularly inspiring. The luminous church hall is arguably even finer. It has a good gift shop and a detailed Mackintosh DVD playing. Garscube Rd is the northern extension of Rose St in the city centre.

when street-food vendors open up stalls and a bar doles out pints to those seeking an escape from the weather. It's family- and dog-friendly. During the week the cafe is still open. (www.facebook.com/platformgla; 253 Argyle St; light meals £4-7; ☻noon-10pm Fri & Sat, to 6pm Sun)

Willow Tearooms   CAFE $

13 🍴 MAP P40, E6

A recreation of the tearooms designed by Charles Rennie Mackintosh in 1904. It backs up its wonderful design elements across a 'white' and a 'blue' room with good teas and reasonable bagels, pastries or, more splendidly, afternoon teas with champagne (£19.95). At busy times the queues for a table can be long. (☑0141-204 5242; www.willowtearooms.co.uk; 97 Buchanan St; light meals £4-8; ☻9am-6.30pm Mon-Sat, 10.30am-5pm Sun; ☎)

Piece   SANDWICHES $

14 🍴 MAP P40, D4

One of a few outlets around town, this basement sandwich shop is run with humour and an upbeat attitude. The sandwiches are really great, with some original fillings and some classics, all bursting with flavour. Sit in at long communal tables or take away. Good coffee too. (☑0141-221 2728; www.pieceglasgow.com; 126 West Regent St; sandwiches £4-5; ☻7.30am-3pm Mon-Fri)

Singl-end   CAFE $$

15 🍴 MAP P40, B3

There's something glorious about this long basement cafe with its cheery service and air of brunchy bonhomie. It coves a lot of bases, with good coffee, generous breakfasts and lunches, booze and baking. Dietary requirements are superbly catered for, with fine vegan choices and clear labelling. On a diet? Avert your eyes from the 'eat-me' cornucopia of meringues and pastries by the door. (☑0141-353 1277; www.thesingl-end.co.uk; 265 Renfrew St; dishes £7-13; ☻9am-5pm; ☎🖉)

Topolabamba   MEXICAN $$

16 ✖ MAP P40, E6

Lots of fun and attractively kitted-out in hipster Mexican decor – all skulls, figurines and tequila crates – this place brings a slice of authentic cuisine to Glasgow, with zingy tacos, tasty tostadas and not a plate of nachos in sight. The stuffed calamari are especially good, but it's all refreshingly flavoursome. Portions are tapa-sized, so order a few and share. (☎0141-248 9359; www.topolabamba.com; 89 St Vincent St; portions £5-11; ☺food noon 10pm Sun Thu, to 10.30pm Fri & Sat; 🛜🍴)

Loon Fung   CANTONESE $$

17 ✖ MAP P40, A3

This elegant Cantonese oasis is one of Scotland's most authentic Chinese restaurants; indeed, it's quite a surprise after a traditional dining experience here to emerge to boisterous Sauchiehall St rather than Hong Kong. The dim-sum choices are toothsome, and the seafood – try the sea bass – really excellent. (☎0141-332 1240; www.loonfungglasgow.com; 417 Sauchiehall St; mains £11-15; ☺noon-11pm; 🛜🍴)

Red Onion   BISTRO $$

18 ✖ MAP P40, D4

This comfortable split-level bistro serves food all day and buzzes with contented chatter. French, Mediterranean and Asian touches add intrigue to the predominantly British menu, and a good-value ixed-price deal is available at weekday lunchtimes.

Topolabamba

(☎0141-221 6000; www.red-onion.co.uk; 257 West Campbell St; mains £13-20; ⏰noon-11pm; 🛜👪)

Bar Soba

ASIAN $$

19 ❌ MAP P40, E6

With candles flickering in windows, there's a certain sense of intimacy in stylish Bar Soba, where industrial meets plush. A great stop in the heart of the shopping zone for lunch; both the bar and downstairs restaurant do quality Asian fusion. Background beats are also perfect for chilling with a cocktail. (☎0141-204 2404; www.barsoba.co.uk; 11 Mitchell Lane; mains £10-13; ⏰food noon-10pm; 🛜)

Meat Bar

AMERICAN $$

20 ❌ MAP P40, D4

Like a mafia-film speakeasy where some minor henchman gets whacked, Meat Bar has under-world ambience carried off with style. As the name suggests, it's all about meat here: it even makes its way into some of the cocktails. Daily cuts of prime Scottish beef (£25 to £40) accompany a range of American-style slow-smoked meats. Tasty and atmospheric, with interesting beers. (☎0141-204 3605; www.themeatbar.co.uk; 142 West Regent St; mains £9-20; ⏰food noon-10pm; 🛜)

Glasgow Tips

o The Glaswegian accent can be tough to understand at first, even for native English speakers. Don't be afraid to ask someone to speak more slowly; locals know that they can be incomprehensible to the uninitiated.

o Glasgow can be quite wet: check the weather forecast and try to plan your museum visits for the rainy spells, saving the parks and strolling for sunnier moments.

o On local buses, drivers aren't generally able to give change, so keep some coins handy for the fare.

o Check out the Tickets Scotland website for medium- and big-name upcoming gigs. It also has a sales office in the city centre with a lengthy gig list on the door.

o Make sure you check out a band in a pub at some point; an essential Glasgow experience.

The Pot Still (p50)

Gamba

SEAFOOD $$$

21 ⊗ MAP P40, D5

This business-district basement is easily missed but is actually one of the city's premier seafood restaurants. Presentation is elegant, with carefully selected flavours allowing the fish, sustainably sourced from Scotland and beyond, to shine. Service is smart and solicitous. There's a good weekday lunch deal, costing £20/22 for two/three courses. (☏ 0141-572 0899; www.gamba.co.uk; 225a West George St; mains £21-30; ⊙ noon-2.15pm & 5-9.30pm Mon-Sat, 5-9pm Sun; 🛜)

Drinking

Sub Club

CLUB

22 ☺ MAP P40, E7

Scotland's most famous house club is still going strong several decades on. Saturdays at the Sub Club are one of Glasgow's legendary nights out, offering serious clubbing with a sound system that aficionados usually rate as the city's best. The claustrophobic, last-one-in vibe is not for those faint of heart. Check the website for details of other nights. (☏ 0141-248 4600; www.subclub.co.uk; 22 Jamaica St; ⊙ typically 11pm-3am Tue, Fri & Sat)

RICHARD WAYMAN/ALAMY STOCK PHOTO ©

Buff Club

The Pot Still PUB

23 🍺 MAP P40, E5

The cheeriest and cosiest of places, The Pot Still has a time-warp feel with its creaky floor and old-style wrought-iron-legged tables. There's a superb whisky selection and knowledgeable staff – constantly up and down ladders to get at bottles – to back it up. Tasty pies (£4) are on hand for solid sustanance. (📞0141-333 0980; www.thepotstill.co.uk; 154 Hope St; ⏱11am-midnight; 📶)

Shilling Brewing Co MICROBREWERY

24 🍺 MAP P40, E5

Drinking in former banks is a Glasgow thing and this central brewpub offers some of the best of it. The wooden, high-ceilinged space has huge windows out to the city centre and room to spare to try its beers; the almost grapefruity Unicorn IPA is a real palate cleanser. Another couple of dozen taps showcase guest craft brews from around Scotland. (📞0141-353 1654; www.shillingbrewingcompany.co.uk; 92 West George St; ⏱noon-11pm Mon, to midnight Tue-Thu, to 1am Fri & Sat, 12.30-11pm Sun; 📶)

Laboratorio Espresso CAFE

25 ☕ MAP P40, E5

A chic space, all concrete and glass, this cafe offers the best coffee we've tried in Glasgow. It's sourced properly, and served in delicious double-shot creations with authentically concentrated espresso, and there's soy milk available. There are a couple of tables outside even in the coldest weather. Pastries and biscotti are on hand, but it's all about the brew here. (📞0141-353 1111; www.labespr.tumblr.com; 93 West Nile St; ⏱7.30am-5.30pm Mon-Fri, from 9am Sat, from 11am Sun)

Buff Club CLUB

26 🍸 MAP P40, C4

Tucked away in a laneway behind the Bath St bar strip, this club presents eclectic, honest music without dress pretensions. The sounds vary substantially depending on the night, and can range from hip-hop to disco via electronica. It's more down to earth than many Glasgow venues, and has seriously cheap drinks midweek.

(☎0141-248 1777; www.thebuffclub. com; 142 Bath Lane; ⊙11pm-3am Mon, Tue & Thu-Sat; 🛜)

MacSorley's PUB

27 🚇 MAP P40, D8

There's nothing better than a good horseshoe-shaped bar in Glasgow, and here the elegantly moulded windows and ceiling add a touch of class to this happy place, which offers live music nightly; check its Facebook page for the week's line-up. (☎0141-222 2288; www.facebook. com/macsorleys1899; 42 Jamaica St; ⊙noon-midnight Mon-Sat, from 12.30pm Sun; 🛜)

Tiki Bar & Kitsch Inn BAR

28 🚇 MAP P40, C4

Hawaiian shirts, palms and leis provide an appropriate backdrop

to colourful cocktails in this hedonistic and amiable basement bar. Upstairs, Kitsch plays the relative straight man, though *MAD* magazine covers mean it's not all poker faces. It also does a good line in Thai food. Order top-shelf spirits to watch the bar staff negotiate the ladder. (☎0141-332 1341; www.tikibarglasgow.com; 214 Bath St; ⊙Kitsch 11am-midnight, Tiki 3pm-midnight Mon-Fri, from 5pm Sat & Sun; 🛜)

Butterfly & the Pig PUB

29 🚇 MAP P40, D4

A breath of fresh air, this offbeat spot makes you feel comfortable as soon as you plunge into its basement depths. The decor is eclectic with a cosy retro feel. There's regular live jazz or similar

MacSorley's

and a sizeable menu – if you can decipher it – of pub grub, plus a rather wonderful tearoom upstairs, great for breakfast before the pub opens. (📞0141-221 7711; www.thebutterflyandthepig.com; 153 Bath St; ⏰11am-1am Mon-Thu, to 3am Fri & Sat, 12.30pm-midnight Sun; 📶)

Classic Grand CLUB

30 🚇 MAP P40, E7

Rock, industrial, electronic and powerpop grace the stage and the turntables at this unpretentious central venue. It doesn't take itself too seriously, drinks are cheap and the locals are welcoming. Hours vary according to events, but core opening is 11pm to 3am Thursday to Saturday. (📞0141-847 0820; www.classicgrand.com; 18 Jamaica St; ⏰hours vary; 📶)

Waterloo Bar PUB, GAY

31 🚇 MAP P40, C7

This traditional pub is Scotland's oldest gay bar. It attracts punters of all ages. It's very friendly and, with a large group of regulars, a good place to meet people away from the scene. (📞0141-248 7216; www.facebook.com/waterloobar1; 306 Argyle St; ⏰noon-11pm Mon-Thu, to midnight Fri & Sat, 12.30-11pm Sun)

Nice 'n' Sleazy BAR, CLUB

32 🚇 MAP P40, A3

On the rowdy Sauchiehall strip, students from the nearby School of Art make the buzz here reliably friendly. If you're over 35, you'll feel like a professor not a punter, but retro decor, a big selection of tap and bottled beers, 3am closing and nightly alternative live music downstairs followed by a club at weekends make this a winner. (📞0141-333 0900; www.nicensleazy.com; 421 Sauchiehall St; ⏰noon-3am Mon-Sat, from 1pm Sun; 📶)

Horse Shoe PUB

33 🚇 MAP P40, E6

This legendary city pub and popular meeting place dates from the late 19th century and is largely unchanged. It's a picturesque spot, with the longest continuous bar in the UK, but its main attraction is what's served over it – real ale and good cheer. Upstairs in the lounge is some of the best-value pub food (dishes £4 to £10) in town. (📞0141-248 6368; www.thehorseshoebarglasgow.co.uk; 17 Drury St; ⏰10am-midnight Sun-Fri, from 9am Sat)

Cathouse CLUB

34 🚇 MAP P40, E7

It's mostly rock, alternative and metal with a touch of Goth and post-punk at this long-standing indie venue. There are two dance floors: upstairs is pretty intense with lots of metal and hard rock; downstairs is a little more tranquil. Admission ranges from free to £6. (📞0141-248 6606; www.cathouse.co.uk; 15 Union St; ⏰10.30pm-3am Wed-Sun; 📶)

Waxy O'Connor's (p54)

TREASUREGALORE/SHUTTERSTOCK ©

Flying Duck BAR

35 MAP P40, E3

Venture down the graffiti-splashed stairs to this bohemian basement space, where there's a sociable studenty vibe, vegan comfort food and regular bands or club events. (☏0141-564 1450; www.theflyingduck. org; 142 Renfield St; ⊗noon-1am Sun-Thu, to 3am Fri & Sat; ☜)

Drum & Monkey PUB

36 MAP P40, E6

Dark wood and marble columns frame this attractive drinking emporium, peppered with church pews and leather lounge chairs. Its cosy and relaxing vibe makes you want to curl up in an arm-chair with a pint. There's tank beer and several real ales on tap; food isn't gourmet but is on until 10pm. (☏0141-221 6636; www. nicholsonspubs.co.uk; 91 St Vincent St; ⊗noon-11pm Sun-Thu, to midnight Fri & Sat; ☜)

Slouch Bar BAR

37 MAP P40, C4

There's a basement bar for all types on Bath St, with subversive hideaways under brokers' offices and a range of vibes. This one is low-lit and casual but handsomely designed, with an American South feel to the decor, drinks and rock soundtrack. It's got an intriguing spirits selection, more-than-acceptable comfort food and regular live music. (☏0141-221 5518; www.slouch-bar.co.uk; 203 Bath St; ⊗11am-2am; ☜)

Waxy O'Connor's PUB

38 🚇 MAP P40, F5

This lager labyrinth with its fantasy-realm elven treehouse feel could be an Escher sketch brought to life, and it's a cut above most Irish theme pubs. (📞0141-354 5154; www.waxyoconnors.co.uk; 44 West George St; 🕐noon-midnight Mon-Sat, 12.30-11pm Sun; 🛜)

Entertainment

King Tut's
Wah Wah Hut LIVE MUSIC

39 ⭐ MAP P40, B5

One of the city's premier live-music pub venues, hosting bands every night. A staple of the local scene, and a real Glasgow highlight.

(📞0141-221 5279; www.kingtuts.co.uk; 272a St Vincent St; 🕐noon-midnight)

Glasgow Film Theatre CINEMA

40 ⭐ MAP P40, C3

This much-loved three-screener off Sauchiehall St shows art-house cinema and classics. (📞0141-332 6535; www.glasgowfilm.org; 12 Rose St; adult/child £10.50/5.50)

Audio CONCERT VENUE

41 ⭐ MAP P40, D8

In the bowels of Central station, this is an atmospheric venue for regular concerts by touring acts, particularly of the rock and metal varieties. (www.facebook.com/audioglasgow; 14 Midland St)

Glasgow Film Theatre

KAY ROXBY/ALAMY STOCK PHOTO ©

Tickets Scotland   BOOKING SERVICE

42 ⭐ MAP P40, D7

For concerts, a useful booking centre is Tickets Scotland, in the Argyle St tunnel. Its website is a good place to browse upcoming gigs; there's a printed list in the window here too. (📞0141-204 5151; www.tickets-scotland.com; 237 Argyle St; 🕙9am-6pm Mon-Wed & Fri-Sat, to 7pm Thu, 11.30am-5.30pm Sun)

Glasgow Royal Concert Hall   CONCERT VENUE

43 ⭐ MAP P40, F4

A feast of classical music is showcased at this concert hall, the modern home of the Royal Scottish National Orchestra. There are also pop, folk and jazz performances, typically by big-name solo artists. (📞0141-353 8000; www.glasgowconcerthalls.com; 2 Sauchiehall St; 🛜)

Theatre Royal   CONCERT VENUE

44 ⭐ MAP P40, E3

Proudly sporting an eyecatching modern facelift, Glasgow's oldest theatre is the home of Scottish Opera. (📞0844 871 7647; www.glasgowtheatreroyal.org.uk; 282 Hope St)

Centre for Contemporary Arts   ARTS CENTRE

45 ⭐ MAP P40, B3

This chic venue makes terrific use of space and light. It covers visual and performing arts, including movies, talks and galleries. There's a good cafe-bar, too.

Local Experiences 👍

Arty locales Bohemian locals hang out at the **Centre for Contemporary Arts** (p55), where there's an excellent **cafe** (p44), or the **Glasgow Film Theatre** (p54).

Clubbing A night out on the dancefloor is a classic Glasgow experience. The legendary **Sub Club** (p49) still rules the roost, but try the **Buff Club** (p50) if you want a more intimate feel.

Live music The vibe at **King Tut's Wah Wah Hut** (p54) is so Glasgow it's not funny. It's an essential live music stop, but check out **MacSorley's** (p51) and **Nice 'n' Sleazy** (p52) as gig venues too.

(📞0141-352 4900; www.cca-glasgow.com; 350 Sauchiehall St; 🕙10am-midnight Mon-Thu, noon-1am Fri & Sat, to midnight Sun, galleries until 6pm Tue-Sun)

Ivory Blacks   LIVE MUSIC

46 ⭐ MAP P40, D7

Inside Central station, this sweaty, atmospheric space is an unpretentious venue for gigs, which are regular and mostly of the rock and metal variety. (📞07538 463752; www.reverbnation.com/venue/ivory blacks; 56 Oswald St)

King's Theatre

THEATRE

47 ⭐ MAP P40, A3

King's Theatre hosts mainly musicals; on rare occasions there are variety shows, pantomimes and comedies. (☏0844 871 7648; www.atgtickets.com; 297 Bath St)

Cineworld

CINEMA

48 ⭐ MAP P40, E4

Mainstream films, heaps of screens. Book online for discounts. (☏0330 333 4444; www.cineworld.co.uk; 7 Renfrew St; adult/child £11/8)

Shopping

Super Market

MARKET

49 🔒 MAP P40, D7

This twice-monthly market in the atmospheric Arches space inside Central station has a wide selection of stalls covering handcrafts, small independent clothing retailers and vintage gear. Food is on hand courtesy of Platform (p44). (www.theglasgowmarkets.com; 253 Argyle St; donation £1; ⊘11am-5pm 2nd & last Sun of month)

LOVEMusic

MUSIC

50 🔒 MAP P40, F5

An independent record shop that stocks a good selection of vinyl and has regular in-store performances. It covers all bases but is strongest on rock, alternative and punk, with lots of Scottish bands featured. (☏0141-332 2099; www.lovemusic

glasgow.com; 34 Dundas St; ⊘10am-6pm Mon-Sat, noon-5.30pm Sun)

Slanj Kilts

CLOTHING

51 🔒 MAP P40, E5

This upbeat shop is a top spot to hire or buy kilts both traditional and modern, as well as other tartan wear and a range of T-shirts and other accessories. Always worth a look. (☏0141-248 5632; www.slanjkilts.com; 80 St Vincent St; ⊘9.30am-5.30pm Mon-Wed, Fri & Sat, to 6.30pm Thu, 11am-4pm Sun)

Inverarity One to One

WINE

52 🔒 MAP P40, C4

This excellent basement wine shop has some very interesting choices, as well as a nice line in whiskies and gins. (☏0141-221 5121; 185 Bath St; ⊘10am-6pm Mon-Fri)

Adventure 1

SPORTS & OUTDOORS

53 🔒 MAP P40, F5

This friendly, no-frills outdoor shop located along the side of Queen Street station is an excellent place to buy hiking boots, backpacks and military surplus gear. (☏0141-353 3788; www.adventure1.co.uk; 38 Dundas St; ⊘9am-5.30pm Mon-Fri, 9.30am-5pm Sat)

Celtic Shop

CLOTHING

54 🔒 MAP P40, E7

This city-centre venue is your stop for all green-and-white footballing gear and Celtic

John Lewis in Buchanan Galleries shopping centre

memorabilia. There's a larger shop at the stadium (p72) itself and one at the airport. (☎0141-204 1588; www.celticfc.net; 154 Argyle St; ⊙9am-6pm Mon-Sat, 11am-5pm Sun)

Buchanan Galleries
SHOPPING CENTRE

55 🔒 MAP P40, F4

At the junction of Sauchiehall and Buchanan Sts, this sizeable centre has a huge number of contemporary clothing retailers as well as the John Lewis department store. (☎0141-333 9898; www.buchanan galleries.co.uk; Royal Exchange Sq; ⊙9am-7pm Mon-Wed & Fri & Sat, to 8pm Thu, 10am-6pm Sat & Sun; 🛜)

Waterstone's
BOOKS

56 🔒 MAP P40, D4

A major bookshop that also sells guidebooks and street maps of Glasgow. There's a cafe here too. (☎0141-332 9105; www.waterstones. com; 153 Sauchiehall St; ⊙8.30am-8pm Mon-Fri, 9am-7pm Sat, 10am-6pm Sun)

Explore ⊕
East End

The East End includes the city's oldest part around Glasgow Cathedral and traditional districts fast becoming hubs of creative activity. One of these, the Calton, once famous for linen mills, is now one of Britain's poorest areas; it hums with life at its renowned Barras market. It's an historically Catholic area; a major focus of worship is the Celtic FC stadium down the road.

Allow a generous half-day to explore the free attractions around Glasgow Cathedral (p60), including an unhurried walk in the necropolis (p63) and visits to Provand's Lordship (p69) and the intriguing St Mungo's Museum of Religious Life & Art (p64).

Visiting the Barras market (p73) is an essential Glasgow weekend experience that could extend into a leisurely day if you factor in a seafood meal, a leisurely browse of the stalls and shops both traditional and modern-creative, and a look around the People's Palace (p69) or perhaps a home game or stadium tour at Celtic Park (p72).

Thirsty? There are three breweries in the region.

Getting There & Around

🏃 It's a 15-minute walk from George Sq to the cathedral, or 20 to Barras markets.

🚌 Numerous bus services pass near the cathedral, including buses 38 and 57. Other buses service London Rd (e.g. bus 18) and Gallowgate (e.g. bus 2, which also goes to Celtic Park) for the Barras. Jump on bus 41 or 90 for the Dennistoun strip.

East End Map on p68

The Barras (p73) ACPOWER/SHUTTERSTOCK ©

Top Experience 📸

Travel Back in Time at Glasgow Cathedral

One of few Scottish churches to survive the Reformation – the Protestants decided to repurpose it for their own worship – Glasgow's cathedral is a majestic Gothic edifice with noteworthy architectural features. Built on the supposed site of St Kentigern's (Mungo) tomb, it has been closely entwined with the city's history. The necropolis behind it is one of Glasgow's best rambles.

◎ MAP P68, C1

📞 0141-552 6891

www.historicenvironment.scot

Cathedral Sq

🕙 9.30am-5.30pm Mon-Sat, 1-5pm Sun Apr-Sep, 10am-4pm Mon-Sat, from 1pm Sun Oct-Mar

Exterior

The fairly svelte 13th-century Gothic lines of the building are nicely offset by the elegant central tower. Fine tracery can be seen on the windows, particularly at the principal western entrance, used only on special occasions. The doorway is fairly unadorned, with just some blind arching above it. It's worth walking around to the cathedral's other end, where the protruding, heavily buttressed lower church gives the building a bulky asymmetry.

Nave

The nave makes an impact with its height – over 30m – and slender grace. There's some stunning stained glass, most of which is 20th century. Particularly fine is Francis Spear's *The Creation* (1958) above the western door, with Adam and Eve centre stage. The aisles, separated by graceful arcades, are flanked with tombs and war memorials hung with regimental colours. Above the arcades are two further levels of elegant arching. The roof is 20th century but conserves some original timber.

Eastern End

The eastern end of the church is divided from the western nave by a harmonious late-15th-century stone choir screen, or pulpitum, with a central door topped by a balustrade. It's decorated with seven characterful pairs of figures that may represent the seven deadly sins. Going through it, you are confronted with a splendid vista of the choir stalls leading to the four narrow lancet windows of the eastern end. These are also evocative works by Francis Spear that depict the Apostles. In the northeastern corner of this area is the upper chapterhouse, a mostly 15th-century space used as a sacristy. The University of Glasgow was founded here in 1451; larger premises were soon built for it.

★ Top Tips

o There are helpful guides throughout the cathedral; don't hesitate to speak to them, as they can point out some interesting details.

o There's no toilet in the necropolis or the cathedral; pop into St Mungo's museum if you're caught short.

o Entry is free but donations for upkeep are appreciated.

✖ Take a Break

Down the hill past the necropolis, Drygate (p71) is a top craft brewery that does all-day food.

Lower Church

This vaulted crypt is an atmospheric space with thick pillars. There's a modern altar over the supposed location of the tomb of St Kentigern/Mungo, a 6th-to-7th-century figure who is the city's patron. His legend grew in the 11th and 12th centuries and his tomb became a major medieval pilgrimage destination. This area was built in the mid-13th century to provide a more fitting setting for the saint's resting place.

On display is some of the fine 19th-century stained glass from Munich that once adorned the windows but was removed in the 20th century, probably because it was fading.

The sunken ambulatory at the eastern end has four square chapels separated by arches; this area featured as L'Hôpital des Anges in Paris in season two of *Outlander*. The tomb of Bishop Wishart, a key supporter of Robert the Bruce and an important figure in the cathedral's construction, is here. The southernmost chapel has a well that was likely venerated before the cathedral was even built and perhaps even before Christianity came to the area.

There's also a lower chapterhouse here, usually closed off by a grille.

Blackadder Aisle

After the gloomy gravitas of the rest of the cathedral, the whiteness here (also spelled Blacader) feels like a dose of light. Though originally this aisle was designed as a crypt for a chapel to be built above, this was never constructed. The tierceron vaulting is spectacular, with ornate ceiling bosses. This was the last part of the cathedral to be built, in the late 15th century.

Necropolis

Once a park, the hill behind the cathedral was converted to a **cemetery** (admission free; ☉7am-4.30pm Apr-Oct, from 8am Nov-Mar) in the 1830s. It is interdenominational; indeed, the first burial was a Jewish man in 1832. It's a spectacular spot for a stroll; there are 50-odd thousand burials here and 3500 monuments, including some designed by Alexander Thomson and Charles Rennie Mackintosh. You reach it via the 'bridge of sighs' that separates the realms of the living and dead; just wander the paths and enjoy the city views and the ornateness of the tombs, built when Glasgow's wealthy captains of industry were at their apogee. At the very top is a monument to John Knox that predates the cemetery. Walking tours run every couple of weeks; check www.glasgownecropolis.org.

Top Experience 📷

Ponder Big Issues at St Mungo's Museum of Religious Life & Art

Across from Glasgow Cathedral, this excellent museum takes an impartial look at world religions through the lenses of cultural objects and art. The overview of how faiths tackle the big questions and experiences of humanity – birth, marriage, death – is fascinating and, while the display is a little dated, this is a brilliant under-the-radar attraction.

◎ MAP P68, C1

📞 0141-276 1625

2 Castle St

admission free

🕙 10am-5pm Tue-Thu & Sat, from 11am Fri & Sun

Gallery of Religious Art

On the 1st floor, this assemblage of stunning pieces of religious art sees a stained-glass John the Baptist and St Michael gazing benevolently over a room with, among other things, a statue of the Buddha, an Indigenous-Australian Dreaming painting, a black-figure Attic vase, Native-American totems, a wooden Kalabari ancestral screen from Nigeria, a standout calligraphic Islamic prayer rug by Ahmed Moustafa and the god Shiva dancing on the demon of ignorance: a fitting symbol for this museum.

Gallery of Religious Life

The 2nd floor is the museum's heart, a compact but immersive space that presents, through photographs and objects, the way different cultures and religions approach major life events. Birth, death, coming of age, sex, marriage, war, the afterlife; it's all looked at here, with perspectives from Benin to British Columbia, from the Day of the Dead to bar mitzvahs. Recorded oral testimony gives the objects context and life.

Third Floor

The top floor has a striking picture window looking out at Glasgow Cathedral and the necropolis, with information on them as well as on the bishop's palace that once stood here (and of which this building is a partial recreation). The exhibition up here covers religion in Scotland, including information on the reformation, missionaries, sectarianism, multiculturalism and the increasingly secular Scottish society. Issues are taken on with text, images and objects, such as contraceptive devices or nasty-looking objects used for corporal punishment of children.

Zen Garden

This Japanese Zen garden was Britain's first, built in 1993. The natural landscape is represented in miniature, with rocks for mountains, gravel for water and grass for land.

★ Top Tips

o The museum also works well if you start on the top floor and work your way down.

o It's quite popular with school groups, but you've got the cathedral and Provand's Lordship to see here too, so you can work your visit around these busy times.

✗ Take a Break

There's a cafe in the museum.

Head down the hill for the really tasty fare at McCune Smith (p71).

Walking Tour 🚶

A Stroll to the Barras

The weekend Barras markets bring Glaswegians down to the East End in numbers. It's a traditional, working-class part of Glasgow and the markets blend that heritage with a few rascals on the make, some glorious vintage shops, and a posse of thoroughly modern creatives doing design and sustainable seafood. It's a great snapshot of the city.

Walk Facts

Start Argyle St, S St Enoch

End Gallowgate, 🚌 2

Length 2.5 kilometres, 2-3 hours

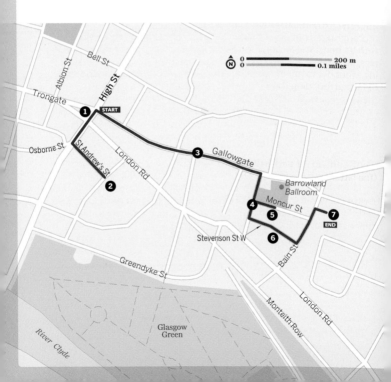

❶ Glasgow Cross

Start your stroll at **Glasgow Cross** (p90). This is where the East End of the city begins, with two of its major arteries, London Rd and Gallowgate, commencing here. The clock tower was once part of the old Tolbooth, or town hall, while the structure topped by a unicorn is the Mercat Cross, where royal decree mandated that a market could be held.

❷ St Andrews

Take a detour to this handsome **church** (p70), tucked off major thoroughfares but quite a sight with its neoclassical columns and elegant steeple. It's worth walking around it to appreciate the detail surrounding the windows, the stately balustrade and the harmonious proportions of the building, now a cultural centre.

❸ Road to the Barras

Along **London Rd and Gallowgate** (the latter a slightly more interesting stroll) is the typical East End mixture of traditional cafes, Polish delis, kebab vendors, mobile-phone mechanics and Celtic pubs sporting Irish flags. If the international chains of Buchanan St are one facet of globalisation, this is the same phenomenon at a family level; it's a gloriously multicultural part of the city.

❹ Barras Markets

The Barras (p73) preserves a democratic old-time feel in its no-nonsense stalls, traditional cafes and the feeling that some of the wares fell off the back of a truck. Check out the down-at-heel second-hand market under the Barrowland Ballroom, a brilliant old dance hall that is one of Britain's most iconic music venues.

❺ The New Barras

In the heart of the Barras area, **Barras Art & Design** (p73) has given a fresh impetus to the markets with its pop-up stalls, excellent seafood restaurant and regular weekend events. It's quite a contrast to the rest of the markets but it works very well.

❻ Vintage Shopping

Disguised by a rather unremarkable facade, the paradise of the past that is **Randall's Antique & Vintage Centre** (p75) has some two-dozen vendors peddling an excellent range of vintage objects. Delving into times gone by makes for an addictive browse.

❼ A Converted Church

There are numerous pubs around here, some of them quite earthy. **St Luke's & the Winged Ox** (p72) is quite a contrast with its organ and stained glass. There are often markets here on Sundays.

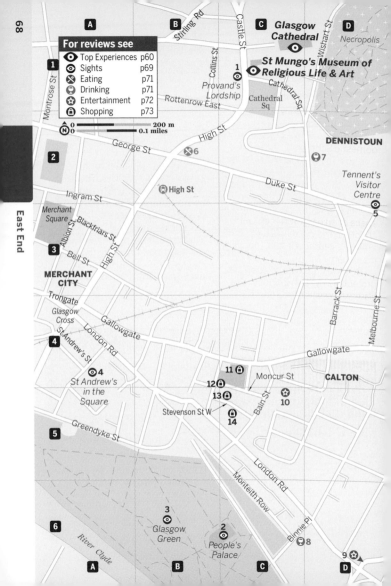

East End

For reviews see
- ⊙ Top Experiences p60
- ⊙ Sights p69
- ⊗ Eating p71
- 🍷 Drinking p71
- 🎭 Entertainment p72
- 🛍 Shopping p73

A · **B** · **C** Glasgow Cathedral ⊙ · **D** Necropolis

Stirling Rd · Castle St · Wishart St

St Mungo's Museum of Religious Life & Art ⊙

Montrose St · Collins St · Provand's Lordship 1 · Cathedral Sq · Cathedral St

1

Rottenrow East · High St

2 George St · ⊗6

🚇 High St · Duke St · DENNISTOUN · 🍷7

Tennent's Visitor Centre 5 ⊙

Ingram St

Merchant Square · Blackfriars St · Albion St · Bell St

3

MERCHANT CITY

Trongate · Gallowgate · Barrack St · Melbourne St

Glasgow Cross · London Rd

4 St Andrew's St · ⊙4 St Andrew's in the Square

Gallowgate

CALTON

11 🛍 · Moncur St
12 🛍
13 🛍 · Bain St · 🎭10
Stevenson St W · 🛍14

5 Greendyke St

London Rd · Monteith Row · Binnie Pl

6 River Clyde · 3 ⊙ Glasgow Green · 2 ⊙ People's Palace · 🍷8 · 9 🎭

A · **B** · **C** · **D**

Ⓝ 0 ___ 200 m
0 ___ 0.1 miles

Sights

Provand's Lordship

HISTORIC BUILDING

1 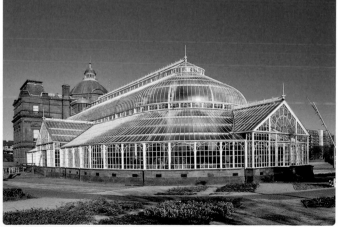 MAP P68, C1

Near the cathedral is Provand's Lordship, the oldest house in Glasgow. A rare example of 15th-century domestic Scottish architecture, it was built in 1471 as a manse. The ceilings and doorways are low, and the rooms are furnished with period furniture and artefacts; upstairs a room recreates the living space of an early-16th-century chaplain. The building's biggest draw is its authentic feel, though it's a shame the original wooden floors have had to be covered for protection. (✆0141-276 1625; www.glasgowmuseums.com; 3 Castle St; admission free; ⊘10am-5pm Tue-Thu & Sat, from 11am Fri & Sun)

People's Palace

MUSEUM

2 MAP P68, C6

Set in the city's oldest park, Glasgow Green, is the solid orange stone People's Palace. It is an impressive museum of social history, telling the story of Glasgow from 1750 to the present through creative, inventive family-friendly displays. The palace was built in the late 19th century as a cultural centre for Glasgow's East End. The attached greenhouse, the **Winter Gardens** (open from 10am to 4.45pm daily), has tropical plants and is a nice spot for a coffee. (✆0141-276 0788; www.glasgow museums.com; Glasgow Green; admission free; ⊘10am-5pm Tue-Thu & Sat, from 11am Fri & Sun)

East End Sights

Winter Gardens greenhouse, People's Palace

DAVID WOODS/SHUTTERSTOCK ©

Glasgow Green
PARK

3 👁 MAP P68, B6

Established by the Bishop of Glasgow in the mid-15th century, this likeable flat green space draped along the Clyde is Glasgow's oldest park. It's a venue for strollers, dog walkers and summer festivals. The obelisk in the middle commemorates Nelson and the victory at Trafalgar.

St Andrew's in the Square
CHURCH

4 👁 MAP P68, A4

This neo-classical Georgian church is quite a sight with its facade of Corinthian columns, tall slender tower and brick-edged windows. The design was based on St Martin-in-the-Fields in London but this is even handsomer. It held its last service in the 1990s and is now a cultural centre. There's a cafe in the undercroft. (☎0141-559 5902; www.facebook.com/saintsglasgow; 1 St Andrew's Sq)

Tennent's Visitor Centre
BREWERY

5 👁 MAP P68, D2

Despite these days of crafty beers and boutique microbreweries, one in every three pints drunk in Scotland is still Tennent's, and that's a lot of pints. Over two hundred million litres are produced here yearly. Fun, comprehensive 90-minute tours of this historic brewery run daily. It's best

Paisley Abbey

If you like Glasgow Cathedral, then you may well want to visit **Paisley Abbey** (☎0141-889 7654; www.paisleyabbey.org.uk; Abbey Close; admission free; ⏰10am-3.30pm Mon-Sat), well worth the short trip from Glasgow. This majestic Gothic building was founded in 1163 by Walter Fitzalan, first high steward of Scotland and ancestor of the Stuart dynasty. Apart from the magnificent perspective down the nave, points of interest include royal tombs, some excellent 19th- and 20th-century stained glass, including three windows by Edward Burne-Jones, and the 10th-century Celtic Barochan Cross.

A monastery for Cluny monks, it was damaged by fire during the Wars of Independence in 1306 but rebuilt soon after. Most of the nave is 14th or 15th century. The building was mostly a ruin from the 16th century until its restoration, started in the 19th century and completed in 1928. A window commemorates the fact that William Wallace was educated by monks from this monastery.

Trains run from Glasgow Central station to Paisley (£3.60, 10 minutes, eight hourly).

TREASUREGALORE/SHUTTERSTOCK ©

Paisley Abbey

to prebook by phone or online. No under-12s are allowed. (📞0141-202 7145; www.tennentstours.com; 161 Duke St; adult/12-18yr £10/8; ⏰9am-6pm Mon-Fri, from 10am Sat & Sun)

Eating

McCune Smith

CAFE $

6 🍴 MAP P68, B2

This stellar cafe is named after a University of Glasgow graduate who was a noted abolitionist and the first African American to hold a medical degree. The hospitable owners take their coffee seriously and offer scrumptious breakfast and brunch fare, plus delicious sandwiches and soups in a luminous, high-ceilinged interior. They bake their own bread and half the

menu or more is vegan. (📞0141-548 1114; www.mccunesmith.co.uk; 3 Duke St; light meals £4-8; ⏰8am-4pm; 📶)

Drinking

Drygate

MICROBREWERY

7 🍺 MAP P68, D2

Dwarfed by the lager megabrewery Tennents next door, Drygate is a proud craft brewery that makes a tempting East End pit stop. You can watch the beer being made on the factory floor as you sip one of two dozen on tap in the likeably convivial, industrially fitted interior or hit the excellent terrace. Burgers, sandwiches, fish and chips and more provide ballast. (📞0141-212 8815; www.drygate.com; 85 Drygate; ⏰11am-midnight; 📶)

West on the Green

BREWERY

8 🚇 MAP P68, C6

Something a bit different, this welcoming and spacious brewpub on the edge of Glasgow Green churns out beers brewed to the traditional German purity laws (which basically means they're bloody good) in a bizarrely ornate former carpet factory opposite the People's Palace. German dishes such as sausages and schnitzel (mains from £10 to £17) can accompany your tipple. There's a great grassy beer garden outside, too. (📞0141-550 0135; www.westonthegreen.com; Binnie Pl; ⏰11am-11pm Sun-Thu, to midnight Fri & Sat; 🛜)

Entertainment

Celtic FC

FOOTBALL

9 ⭐ MAP P68, D6

Playing in green and white hoops, Celtic are one of Glasgow's big two football clubs and traditionally represent the Catholic side of the divide. There are daily stadium tours (adult/child £12.50/7.50). Catch either the bus 61 or 62 from outside St Enoch centre. (📞0871 226 1888; www.celticfc.net; Celtic Park, Parkhead)

St Luke's & the Winged Ox

LIVE MUSIC

By the Barras market area (see 1 🅐 Map p68, C5), this repurposed church – the stained

Celtic Park stadium, home to Celtic FC

glass and organ are still in situ – is a fantastic spot hosting live music every weekend, exhibitions, markets and more. The cosier attached space also does very well just as a pub and serves food all day until 9pm. (📞0141-552 8378; www.stlukes glasgow.com; 17 Bain St; ⊘noon-midnight; 🛜)

Barrowland Ballroom

CONCERT VENUE

10 ⭐ MAP P68, C4

A down at heel but exceptional old dancehall above the Barras market catering for some of the larger acts that visit the city. It's one of Scotland's most atmospheric venues with its sprung floor and authentic character. (The Barrowlands; www.glasgow-barrowland.com; 244 Gallowgate)

Shopping

The Barras

MARKET

11 🔒 MAP P68, C4

Glasgow's legendary weekend flea market, the Barras on Gallowgate, is a fascinating mixture of on-trend openings and working-class Glasgow. Old stalls flogging time-faded glasses, posters and DVDs that you'd struggle to give away are juxtaposed with vintage classics, very earthy traders' pubs and a street scene where fake designer gear is marked down and dodgy characters peddle smuggled cigarettes. (📞0141-552 4601; www. glasgow-barrowland.com; btwn Gallowgate & London Rd; ⊘10am-5pm Sat & Sun)

Barras Art & Design

ARTS & CRAFTS

12 🔒 MAP P68, C5

This workshop zone for artists and designers in the heart of the Barras has helped pep up the area

The Old Firm and Sectarianism

One of world football's most passionate and bitter rivalries divides Glasgow; when Celtic and Rangers, known as the Old Firm, take to the field they aren't just disputing a league or a cup but in part playing out old rivalries between Catholics and Protestants, between Ireland and Britain, between establishment and rebellion, between Celt and Anglo-Saxon.

Though the clubs themselves have abandoned sectarian recruiting of players, Celtic traditionally represent the city's Catholic population, which was boosted by mass immigration from Ireland through the late 19th and early 20th centuries. Playing in green and white hoops and with a shamrock for a badge, they are passionately followed in Ireland as well as Scotland.

Rangers, meanwhile, decked out in royal blue, traditionally represent Protestants. They are the team of choice for many who wish to conserve Northern Ireland's union with Britain and Scotland's with England.

Little wonder then that the atmosphere at the games can be heated. Aggressively sectarian songs recall events as far back as the Battle of the Boyne in 1690 but also the more recent Troubles in Northern Ireland. Losing cannot be countenanced and the simmering passions in the stands are often played out on the pitch in high-tempo, aggressive encounters. With at least four meetings every season, there's not much time for passions to die down until the next instalment.

The size and support of the two clubs has led to their dominance of Scottish football; indeed, many smaller teams rely on their fixtures with the Old Firm in order to keep afloat. Between them, they have won more than 100 league championships and more than 100 Scottish and League Cups. They have met more than 400 times with a very even spread of results, though long periods of dominance of one or the other have regularly occurred.

A financial scandal in 2012 that led to Rangers' liquidation saw the formation of a new company and the club having to work its way back up to the top flight from the lowest division. Some Celtic supporters provocatively insist that Rangers don't exist any more; yet more grist to the rivalry mill!

and bring a new wave of folk in. It's a lovely covered courtyard with a bar, cafe and restaurant, as well as pop-up and other shops. There are events on most weekends, including a monthly farmers market. (BAaD; ☎0141-237 9220; www.baadglasgow.com; Moncur St; ☉noon-midnight Tue-Sat, 11am-10pm Sun)

Randall's Antique & Vintage Centre

VINTAGE

13 🔒 MAP P68, C5

This is a real treasure trove of the once loved, the tacky, the tawdry, the magnificent and the curious from the not-so-recent past. It's an excellent set-up with several sellers and a top spot to browse. Don't take the kids; they'll make you feel ancient with their incredulity at items that you remember using not so very long ago. (☎07752 658045; www.facebook.com/randalls

Eastern Sleeps

There aren't many standout sleeping options in the East End, but it's easy to walk here from digs in Merchant City or the eastern end of Central Glasgow.

antiqueandvintagecentre; Stevenson St West; ☉9am-5pm Sat & Sun)

Braw Wee Emporium

GIFTS & SOUVENIRS

14 🔒 MAP P68, C5

Occupying a corner of Barras Art & Design, this quirky shop lives up to its name with a range of offbeat gifts and a well-curated musical selection. (☎0141-237 4270; www.braw-wee-emporium.com; Stevenson St West; ☉noon-6pm Wed-Fri, 10.30am-5.30pm Sat & Sun)

Explore ✦
Merchant City

What was once the domain of sober industrialists, whose palaces of trade and commerce dignify the area, Merchant City is now a playground of restaurants, bars and shops. It's an atmospheric zone that rewards idle strolling with handsome facades and quirky architectural details. Come night-time, there's a buzzy vibe as the area fills with social life and the knot of LGBTIQ+ venues known as the Pink Triangle starts to hum.

Pacing around on foot is the best way to get to grips with this area, which is better appreciated as an architectural ensemble than as a list of must-see attractions. Start your exploration at George Square (p90), where the free guided tour of the City Chambers (p78) is a highlight, and then delve into the narrow streets to the south and east. Remember to look up at the facades of the buildings you are passing; many were trade guilds, mercantile exchanges, shipping company offices or organs of state.

Getting There & Around
🚌 From the West End, bus 6 is a useful service to get you here.

S Buchanan Street and St Enoch are the closest subway stops.

🚌 Queen Street station is very handy.

Merchant City Map on p88

City Chambers (p78) JEFF WHYTE/SHUTTERSTOCK ©

Top Experience 📷

Walk Through the Corridors of Power at City Chambers

Glasgow's impressive town hall dominates the eastern end of George Sq. It was built in the 1880s in a French-inspired blend of neoclassical and neo-Renaissance architecture and was opened by Queen Victoria in 1888 after going five times over budget. Most of the interior is only accessible by a free guided tour that leaves twice daily on weekdays.

◉ MAP P88, E1

📞 0141-287 2000

www.glasgow.gov.uk

George Sq

admission free

🕑 9am-5pm Mon-Fri

Foyer

The foyer, accessible to the public during opening hours, is an impressive space, with polished red granite columns, caryatids glistening with mica and elaborate mosaic work on the floor and ceiling; a real artisanal labour recalling Glasgow's former preeminence as a port city. The city's coat of arms underfoot features two fish flanking objects related to deeds of St Mungo, who is represented above. In the foyer there's also a war memorial lamp and the benevolent gaze of a bust of Nelson Mandela.

Staircases

The twin three-level staircases in various Carrara marbles and alabaster are a majestic feature and one of the main reasons why the building cost so much; some of the panels had to be painted to resemble marble to get it over the line. Look out for Clyde, the perky thistle-shaped 2014 Commonwealth Games mascot, at the base of the right-hand staircase. On the left-hand one, rub the lion's nose for luck as generations of council staff have done before you.

Council Chamber

The city council only meets here every six weeks, so you can normally enter. It's a stunning space decked out in handcarved Spanish mahogany. Sit at one of the councillors' very comfortable red leather seats, which are arranged in a semicircle in front of the Lord Provost's throne. In front of that is a holder for the ceremonial mace, while at either end of the room are ornate fireplaces topped by the coat of arms. Above is a small public gallery.

Banqueting Hall

Over 50ft high, the main banqueting hall is suitably imposing. The red patterned carpet reflects the pattern of the fine coffered ceiling; the brass

★ **Top Tips**

o The free guided tours run from Monday to Friday at 10.30am and 2.30pm; pop in earlier in the day to book your spot.

o Lifts are available if the stairs are an issue.

o If you visit the chambers during Glasgow Doors Open Days Festival in September, you can venture into more of the building, including an elegant library, and have a peek at the impressive ceremonial mace.

✕ **Take a Break**

Wander into Merchant City for a tasty Asian-inflected vegan lunch at Picnic (p91).

chandeliers are best appreciated from the minstrel's gallery above. Mural and canvas paintings by several of the Glasgow Boys movement line the hall, with depictions of arts and crafts, the virtues, the rivers Tay, Forth, Clyde and Tweed, and paintings of St Mungo, shipbuilding and the Glasgow fair. Off this hall, a suite of rooms is decorated in various woods and features some fine paintings, including a couple of Hornel works portraying springtime.

Picture Gallery

The top floor is decked out with a series of portraits of Lord Provosts and other Glasgow worthies, under a glass dome. It's interesting to see the varied styles at work as different artists at different times took on their subject. Check out Peter Howson's likeably irreverent portrait of Pat Lally, a resilient Labour politician and notable Glasgow figure of the last decades of the 20th century.

Did You Know?

Nelson Mandela was given the freedom of the city by Glasgow in 1981; it was the first city to do so and it was a significant boost to the imprisoned activist.

Exterior

The building's imposing four-storey main facade made a powerful statement about Glasgow's wealth when it was erected and is still impressive. A sober Italianate design, it incorporates both neoclassical and neo-baroque elements and is backed by a soaring bell tower that has a churchy air. Elegant Venetian windows run along the higher floors, flanked on the top level by sculptures representing the worthy ideals of the age.

Top Experience 📷
Watch a Show at Sharmanka Kinetic Theatre

Glasgow's most unusual sight is tucked away upstairs in an arts centre, but make sure you track it down to see a show. Meeting the deeply strange and wondrous creations of Eduard Bersudsky, a sculptor and mechanic, is a real privilege for adults and children alike. You'll run the gamut of emotions and marvel at this strange and wonderful world.

◎ MAP P88, F4

www.sharmanka.com

103 Trongate, G1 5HD

🕑 For show times, prices and to book tickets visit: www.ticketsource.co.uk/sharmanka

Background

Bersudsky moved to Scotland in the 1990s from Russia, where he had already begun creating his 'kinemats'. These are extraordinarily detailed and delightful mechanical sculptures crafted from scrap metal and elaborately carved wood, fitted with motors and, it seems, a soul. Each one performs a story set to music; these are sometimes humorous, sometimes deeply sad but always acutely wry commentaries on the human condition. They often focus on Russian themes.

Self-Portrait with Monkey

With its lugubrious face, body of linked chains and horned head, this is one of the most poignant sculptures. Sharmanka means 'barrel organ' and this figure turns a wringer while a Russian song of loss plays and it taps its booted feet. A monkey swings from a pendulum between them. It's not hard to feel the artist's sense of loss and sadness about his self-imposed exile from Russia.

Rag 'n' Bone Man

The artist has often sourced his materials from nearby Barras market, and this curious (to say the least) figure is a tribute to the traders there. With fans for hands, a whir of cogs and typewriter keys for innards, a wise wooden human-animal face with pince-nez, a bell hanging from its nose and a strange figure riding a stuffed loon atop its head, this is one of the most delightful pieces in the collection.

Time of Rats

A sturdy wooden mole with a long nose and a tail and four spiked wheels represents Russia here. All through a structure on its back cavorting rats play with various contraptions: a typewriter, a gramophone, a sewing machine. They represent those who control the artist's homeland.

★ Top Tips

○ Arrive a bit early and examine the sculptures before the show starts; the detail on some of them is amazing.

○ Sharmanka runs a weekly schedule featuring a variety of shows suitable for all ages. For a full description visit: www.sharmanka.com

✕ Take a Break

Head up Candleriggs to Bar 91 (p92) for a decent pub meal

Round the corner, Mono (p91) does good vegan food and has a record store to browse.

Walking Tour 🚶

Merchant City Ramble

This walk introduces you to the historic buildings of Merchant City, built during the 18th century, when the trans-Atlantic tobacco trade brought wealth flooding into the city, and the 19th century, when shipbuilding and textiles kept the industrialists prosperous. Part of the fun of the stroll is seeing the numerous new purposes these creatively refitted buildings are being put to.

Walk Facts

Start Buchanan St;
Ⓢ Buchanan St

End Glasgow Cross;
Ⓢ St Enoch

Length 2km; one hour

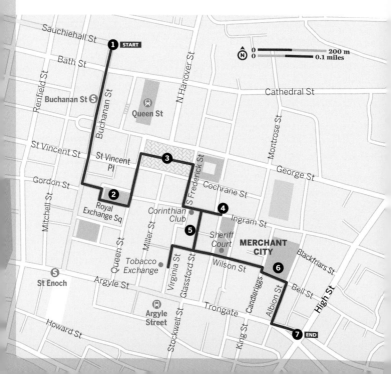

❶ Into the Merchant City

Start at the junction of two major shopping thoroughfares, Sauchiehall and Buchanan Sts, overseen by a bronze **statue** of Donald Dewar, Scotland's inaugural First Minister. Stroll down pedestrian Buchanan St, then left through one of the handsome gateways into stylish Merchant City, once headquarters for Glasgow industrialists.

❷ Modern Art

The strikingly colonnaded **Gallery of Modern Art** (p90) was once the Royal Exchange and now hosts contemporary art displays, with a library and cafe in the basement. Outside, the horseback statue of the Duke of Wellington sports a traffic cone on his head that the authorities finally tired of removing only for it to reappear overnight.

❸ George Square

Turn left up Queen St to **George Square**, surrounded by imposing Victorian architecture, including the grandiose City Chambers. Statues include Robert Burns, James Watt and, atop a Doric column, Sir Walter Scott. Seen *World War Z*? Some of the Pittsburgh scenes were filmed at this spot in Glasgow.

❹ Noble Buildings

Walk down South Frederick St. Ahead of you, former Court House cells now house the **Corinthian Club** (p94); drop into the bar for a glimpse of the extravagant interior, then continue to **Hutcheson's**

Hall (p90). This was built in 1805 as a hospital and school for the poor with a bequest from the brothers whose statues stand in the facade.

❺ Tobacco Traders

Retrace your steps one block and continue south down Glassford St past **Trades Hall** (p90), designed by Robert Adam in 1791. Turn right into Wilson St and left along Virginia St, lined with the old warehouses of the Tobacco Lords; many converted into posh flats. The **Tobacco Exchange** (p90) straddles pretty Virginia Court. Sugar and tobacco were traded here in the 18th and 19th centuries.

❻ Merchant Square

Back on Wilson St, the **Old Sheriff Court** fills a whole block and has been both Glasgow's town hall and main law court. Continue east on Wilson St past Ingram Sq to **Merchant Square**, a covered courtyard that was once the city's fruit market but now bustles with cafes and bars.

❼ Glasgow Cross

Continue strolling to this junction that marks the end of Merchant City and the beginning of the East End. The **Tolbooth Steeple** clock tower was once part of the 17th-century town hall. The nearby **Mercat Cross** is another traditional element of an historic Scottish burgh that indicated the place where a market could be held.

Walking Tour 🚶

Browsing the Style Mile

Glasgow's pedestrianised central streets are devoted to retail and people come from all over Scotland to spend a weekend here refreshing their wardrobes. In truth, most of the stores are familiar British and global chains, but having so many in one concentrated area is what pulls the crowds. Edinburgh may have the Royal Mile, but Glasgow's got the Style Mile.

Walk Facts

Start Gallery of Modern Art; Ⓢ Buchanan St

End Buchanan Galleries; Ⓢ Buchanan St

Length 1.5km; two hours

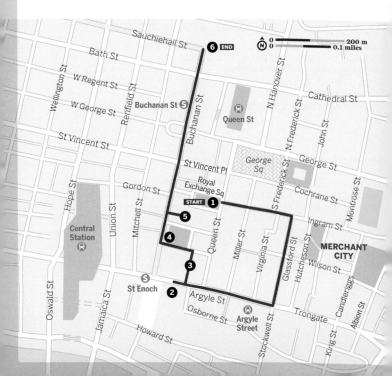

❶ Ingram Street

Start your journey outside the **Gallery of Modern Art** (p90). The Duke of Wellington with a traffic cone on his head points the way down Ingram St. In the first couple of blocks you'll find plenty of upmarket shops like Ralph Lauren, Emporio Armani, Mulberry, Agent Provocateur and Cruise.

❷ Argyle Street

There are some uninspiring shops in the pedestrianised section of Argyle St; eschew those and dive straight into the renovated **St Enoch Centre** (p99). It's a good one for families with Hamley's and a Disney store, but there are lots of high-street favourites too, as well as a Debenhams department store and a cute Glasgow Museums shop.

❸ All That Glitters

Opened in 1827, the beautiful **Argyll Arcade** (p98) runs between Argyle and Buchanan Sts via a 90-degree turn. Take the time to chat with the cheerful top-hatted doorpeople then head in to what is wholly devoted to jewellery and watch retailers. Need a little something that will fit in your carry-on?

Otherwise, it's fun to watch breathless couples choosing wedding rings.

❹ Peacock Palace

With all the finery on offer in the Style Mile, the unmissable peacock facade is an appropriate symbol for the gorgeously renovated historic shopping centre **Princes Square** (p98). Inside, it's all wrought iron and light, with a range of fashion stores including Vivienne Westwood, Ted Baker and French Connection.

❺ Time for a Pit Stop

Princes Square has several places to get off your feet and revive with a meal and a drink, and there are some excellent pubs and cafes for a pit stop just off Buchanan St.

❻ Top of the Hill

Weighed down by your numerous purchases, you stagger up Buchanan St, where it looks like the shops might finally come to an end. But no, here's **Buchanan Galleries** (p57), with a John Lewis and more than 80 other retailers, including Fred Perry, Mango and River Island. Still going? Sauchiehall St runs west from here with even further shopping choice.

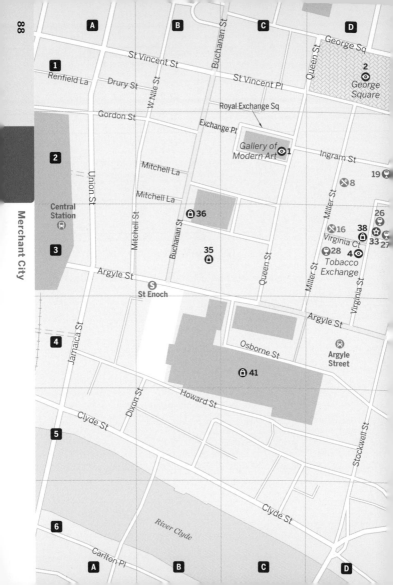

A

B

C

D

1

2

3

4

5

6

George Sq

St Vincent St

Buchanan St

Queen St

George Sq

Renfield La

Drury St

W Nile St

St Vincent Pl

2
George
Square

Gordon St

Royal Exchange Sq

Exchange Pl

Gallery of
Modern Art ⊙1

Ingram St

Central
Station

Mitchell La

Mitchell La

Miller St

19

❽8

26

🔒36

❽16

38
🔒

33

27

35
🔒

28
⊙4

Virginia Ct

Tobacco
Exchange

Argyle St

St Enoch

Union St

Mitchell St

Buchanan St

Queen St

Miller St

Virginia St

Argyle St

Osborne St

Argyle
Street

🔒41

Jamaica St

Dixon St

Howard St

Stockwell St

Clyde St

River Clyde

Clyde St

Carlton Pl

A

B

C

D

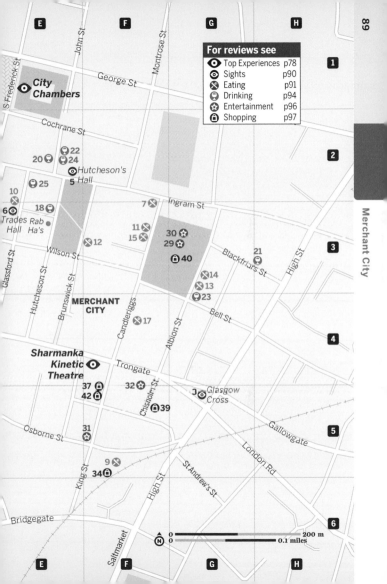

Merchant City

For reviews see

◎	Top Experiences	p78
⊙	Sights	p90
✖	Eating	p91
🍷	Drinking	p94
★	Entertainment	p96
🔒	Shopping	p97

E **F** **G** **H**

John St

George St

Montrose St

S Frederick St

◎ **City Chambers**

Cochrane St

20 🍷 🍷 22
      🍷 24

🍷 25

⊙ Hutcheson's
5 Hall

10
✖
6 ◎ 18 🍷
**Trades
Hall** Rab
Ha's

7 ✖ Ingram St

11 ✖
15 ✖

30 ★
29 ★

🔒 40

21 🍷

Glassford St

Wilson St

✖ 12

Hutcheson St

Brunswick St

**MERCHANT
CITY**

Candleriggs

Albion St

Blackfriars St

High St

✖ 14
✖ 13
🍷 23

Bell St

✖ 17

**Sharmanka
Kinetic** ◎
Theatre

Trongate

37 🔒
42 🔒

32 🔒

Chisholm St

🔒 39

Glasgow
Cross ◎

Gallowgate

Osborne St

31 ★

King St

9 ✖
34 🔒

High St

St Andrew's St

London Rd

Bridgegate

Saltmarket

▲
Ⓝ 0 ——————— 200 m
    0 ————————— 0.1 miles

Sights

Gallery of Modern Art
GALLERY

1 ⊚ MAP P88, C2

This contemporary art gallery features modern works from local and international artists, housed in a graceful neoclassical building. The original interior is an ornate contrast to the inventive art often on display, though quality varies markedly by exhibition. There's also an effort made to keep the kids entertained. Usually the horseback statue of the Duke of Wellington outside is cheekily crowned with a traffic cone; the authorities grumble, but it keeps happening and is now an icon. (GoMA; ☏ 0141-287 3050; www.glasgowmuseums.com; Royal Exchange Sq; admission free; ⏱10am-5pm Mon-Wed & Sat, until 8pm Thu, 11am-5pm Fri & Sun)

George Square
SQUARE

2 ⊚ MAP P88, D1

Stately George Sq is the civic centre of Glasgow, dominated by the town hall – City Chambers (p78) – on the eastern side. The large open space is dignified by statues of famous folk from Glasgow and the surrounding area, including Robert Burns, James Watt and Sir John Moore, and, atop a column, Sir Walter Scott. A pair of charismatic lions guards the war memorial.

Glasgow Cross
SQUARE

3 ⊚ MAP P88, G5

This junction of five roads is a major Glasgow landmark and indicates the end of Merchant City and beginning of the East End. Standing tall is the **Tolbooth Steeple**, a clocktower that is all that remains of the 17th-century town hall. Near it is the **Mercat Cross**, which traditionally marked the place that a market could be held by royal decree, represented here by a unicorn.

Tobacco Exchange
HISTORIC BUILDING

4 ⊚ MAP P88, D3

The solid Tobacco Exchange flanks pretty Virginia Court. Sugar and tobacco were traded here in the 18th and 19th centuries. (Virginia St)

Hutcheson's Hall
HISTORIC BUILDING

5 ⊚ MAP P88, E2

This noble Merchant City edifice was built in 1805 as a hospital and a school for the poor with a bequest from the brothers whose statues stand in the facade. It now holds a restaurant (p94). (158 Ingram St)

Trades Hall
HISTORIC BUILDING

6 ⊚ MAP P88, E3

Designed by Robert Adam in 1791 to house the trades guild, this is one of Merchant City's most notable buildings, with its dignified neoclassical facade and green dome. It's an events space, but someone might be able to show you the interior if you are interested and there's nothing on at the time. (📞0141-552 2418; www.tradeshallglasgow.co.uk; 85 Glassford St; admission free; ⏰9am-5pm Mon-Fri)

Eating

Picnic

VEGAN, CAFE $

7 ❌ MAP P88, F3

Bright and upbeat, this popular lunch stop serves an appealing range of vegan snacks, sandwiches and various Asian-influenced dishes. There's plenty to choose from, and excellent juices and smoothies too. (📞0141-552 8788; www.picnic-cafe.co.uk; 103 Ingram St; light meals £4-8; ⏰8am-4.30pm Mon-Sat, from 10am Sun; 📶🍴)

Paesano Pizza

PIZZA $

8 ❌ MAP P88, D2

This back-to-basics Merchant City choice just off the Ingram St shopping strip is a sizeable restaurant with an open kitchen at the end. The reduced menu does really tasty pizzas in a fairly traditional Neapolitan style. Add some cheap Italian wines, a couple of salads and that's it. Great value. (📞0141-258 4465; www.paesanopizza.co.uk; 94 Miller St; pizzas £6-8; ⏰noon-10.30pm Sun-Wed, to 11pm Thu, to midnight Fri & Sat)

Mono

VEGAN $

9 ❌ MAP P88, F5

Combining vegan food with a music shop, ultra-casual Mono is a boho Glasgow classic. The menu

Duke of Wellington statue and the Gallery of Modern Art

takes on favourites like burgers and fish and chips, as well as a few globally influenced dishes like *banh mi,* jerk jackfruit burritos and falafel wraps. Mono is also a relaxing place for a coffee or a beer. (☏0141-553 2400; www.monocafebar. com; 12 Kings Ct, King St; mains £7-10; ☺food noon-9pm; 🛜🌱)

Soulsa Cafe
CAFE $

10 ✖ MAP P88, E2

Set in the Trades Hall, a notable Merchant City edifice, this very cordial cafe has real soul, with home baking, tasty coffee and a range of dishes inspired by Southern USA. There are regular soul DJs and open mike sessions, as well as live bands. It's also a good spot for a drink or cocktail. (☏0141-552 0262; www.soulsacafebar. co.uk; 87 Glassford St; mains £8-13; ☺10am-midnight)

Bar 91
PUB FOOD $

11 ✖ MAP P88, F3

This happy, buzzy bar serves excellent meals, far better than your average pub food. Salads, pasta and burgers are among the many tasty offerings, and in summer tables spill out onto the sidewalk – ideal for people-watching. (☏0141-552 5211; www.bar91.co.uk; 91 Candleriggs; mains £6-10; ☺meals noon-9pm Mon-Sat, 1-7pm Sun; 🛜)

Brutti Ma Buoni
CAFE $

12 ✖ MAP P88, F3

Casual Brutti is a cafe-bar offering decent food at happily low prices. Italian and Spanish influences give

Paesano Pizza (p91)

rise to tapas-like servings or full-blown meals; it's also a fine spot for a beer, especially when the outdoor terrace is open. The £5 mini dishes make a more-than-decent lunch. (📞 0141-552 0001; www.brunswickhotel.co.uk; 106 Brunswick St; mains £8-11; 🕙 11am-10pm Sun-Thu, to 11pm Fri & Sat, reduced hours Jan & Feb; 🛜 👬)

Café Gandolfi CAFE, BISTRO $$

13 ❌ MAP P88, G3

In Merchant City, this cafe was once part of the old cheese market. It's been pulling in the punters for years and attracts an interesting mix of die-hard Gandolfers, the upwardly mobile and tourists. It covers all the bases with excellent breakfasts and coffee, an enticing upstairs bar (p94), and top-notch bistro food, including Scottish and continental options, in an atmospheric medieval-like setting. (📞 0141-552 6813; www.cafegandolfi.com; 64 Albion St; mains £10-18; 🕙 8am-11pm Mon-Sat, from 9am Sun; 🛜)

Gandolfi Fish SEAFOOD $$

14 ❌ MAP P88, G3

This welcoming and approachable place, with a takeaway outlet alongside, is an offshoot of the ever-popular neighbouring Café Gandolfi (p93). Attractive art and comfortable seats grace a spacious venue, where well-put-together dishes evidence plenty of thought behind the scenes. Scallops are delicious and the

catch of the day is excellent. There's a good two- or three-course menu deal (£13/19) running from lunchtime until early evening. (📞 0141-552 9475; www.cafegandolfi.com; 84 Albion St; mains £13-20; 🕙 noon-11pm Mon-Sat, 10am-9pm Sun)

Dakhin INDIAN $$

15 ❌ MAP P88, F3

This South Indian restaurant is a pleasing change of air from the majority of the city's excellent curry scene. Dishes are from all over the South, and include *dosas* (thin rice-based crêpes) and a yummy variety of fragrant coconut-based curries. If you're really hungry, try a *thali*: an assortment of Indian 'tapas'. The food is all gluten-free. (📞 0141-553 2585; www.dakhin.com; 89 Candleriggs; mains £9-19; 🕙 noon-2pm & 5-11pm Mon-Fri, 1-11pm Sat & Sun; 🛜 🍽)

Spanish Butcher SPANISH $$$

16 ❌ MAP P88, D3

In a refined interior, moodily dark with industrial decor above retro wickerwork chairs, this is a fine venue for quality northern Spanish beef, with the best cuts designed for sharing. But there's plenty more to delight: whole baked fish, expertly deboned, are attractive and succulent, while the *secreto* and *presa* cuts redefine the pork genre. (📞 0141-406 9880; www.spanishbutcher.com; 80 Miller St; mains £16-22; 🕙 noon-1am; 🛜)

Guy's

SCOTTISH $$$

17 🍽 MAP P88, F4

This Merchant City restaurant offers a very authentic Glasgow blend of style and friendly informality, and has a long list of devoted regulars. The buzzing atmosphere and decor – from gilt mirrors to porcelain plates – slightly outdo the food, which is tasty but unremarkable. Drinks are way overpriced and the service, though willing, is painfully slow. But the experience is a worthwhile one. (📞0141-552 1114; www.guysrestaurant.co.uk; 24 Candleriggs; mains £18-28; ⊙noon-10.30pm Mon-Fri, to 11.30pm Sat, 12.30-10.30pm Sun)

Corinthian Club

HEMIS/ALAMY ©

Drinking

DogHouse Merchant City BAR

18 🍺 MAP P88, E3

Brewdog's zingy beers are matched by its upbeat attitude, so this Merchant City spot was always going to be a fun place. An open kitchen doles out slidery, burgery smoked-meat fare while 25 taps run quality craft beer from morning till night. (📞0141-552 6363; www.brewdog.com; 99 Hutcheson St; ⊙11am-midnight Mon-Fri, from 10am Sat & Sun; 🛜)

Bar Gandolfi COCKTAIL BAR

Above the cafe of the same name (see 13 🍽 Map p88, G3), this little upstairs gem is far from the often-boisterous Merchant Sq pubs opposite. Pared-back unvarnished wooden stools and tables, offbeat art exhibitions and a large kitchen-bar area – there's far more space behind it than on the patrons' side – create a relaxing space for a quality cocktail or spirit. There's also tasty, well-sourced food available. (📞0141-552 4462; www.cafegandolfi.com; 64 Albion St; ⊙noon-midnight; 🛜)

Corinthian Club BAR

19 🍺 MAP P88, D2

A breathtaking domed ceiling and majestic chandeliers make this casino a special space. Originally a bank and later Glasgow's High Court, this regal building's main bar is a stunner. Cosy wraparound seating and room to spare are complemented by a restaurant, a nightclub, a piano bar, a roof terrace and a champagne bar, as well as the casino area itself. (📞0141-552 1101; www.thecorinthianclub.co.uk; 191 Ingram St; ⏰11am-2am Sun-Thu, noon-3am Fri & Sat; 📶)

Katie's Bar
GAY & LESBIAN

20 MAP P88, E2

With an easily missed entrance between a Spanish and an Italian restaurant, this basement bar is a friendly LGBTIQ+ pub with a pool table and regular gigs at weekends. It's a pleasant, low-key space to start off the night and especially popular with women. (📞0141-237 3030; www.katiesbar.co.uk; 17 John St; ⏰noon-midnight; 📶)

Babbity Bowster
PUB

21 MAP P88, H3

In a quiet corner of Merchant City, this handsome spot is perfect for a tranquil daytime drink, particularly in the adjoining beer garden. Service is attentive, and the smell of sausages may tempt you to lunch; it also offers accommodation. This is one of the city centre's most charming pubs, in one of its noblest buildings. There's a regular folk-music scene here. (📞0141-552 5055; www.babbitybowster.com; 16-18 Blackfriars St; ⏰11am-midnight Mon-Sat, from 12.30pm Sun; 📶)

Babbity Bowster

Speakeasy
BAR, GAY

22 MAP P88, E2

Relaxed and friendly bar that starts out publike and gets louder with gay anthem DJs as the night progresses. Entry is free and it serves food until 9pm, so it's a good all-rounder. Upstairs from midnight on Saturdays is the Midnight Glory club night (£3). (📞0845 166 6036; www.speakeasy glasgow.co.uk; 10 John St; ⏰5pm-3am Wed-Sat)

Artà
BAR, CLUB

23 MAP P88, G4

Set in a former cheese market, this place is very OTT with its Mediterranean-villa decor; it really does have to be seen to be believed. Despite the luxury, it's got a relaxed, chilled vibe and makes a decent cocktail. It also does Spanish-influenced food but it's better visited as a bar and nightclub. (📞0845 166 6018; www.arta. co.uk; 62 Albion St; ⏰5pm-midnight Thu, to 3am Fri, 12.30pm-3am Sat; 📶)

Underground
BAR, GAY

24 🚇 MAP P88, E2

Downstairs on cosmopolitan John St, Underground sports a relaxed crowd and, crucially, a free jukebox. You'll be listening to indie rather than Abba here. (📞0141-553 2456; www.facebook.com/undergroundglasgo; 6a John St; ⏰noon-midnight; 📶)

AXM
CLUB, GAY

25 🚇 MAP P88, E2

This popular Manchester club's Glasgow branch is a cheery spot, not too scene-y, with all welcome. It's a fun place to finish off a night out. (📞0141-552 5761; www.axmglasgow.com; 80 Glassford St; ⏰11pm-3am Wed & Sun, from 10pm Thu-Sat)

Delmonica's
BAR, GAY

26 🚇 MAP P88, D3

In the heart of the Pink Triangle, this is a popular bar with a good mix of ages and orientations. It packs out in the evenings when bingo, quizzes, drag shows and other fun keep things lively, and it's a pleasant spot for a quiet drink during the day. Come here before the adjacent Polo Lounge, as you might get a free pass.

(📞0141-552 4803; www.delmonicas. co.uk; 68 Virginia St; ⏰noon-midnight Mon-Sat, from 12.30pm Sun)

Polo Lounge
CLUB, GAY

27 🚇 MAP P88, D3

One of the city's principal gay clubs is an attractive spot, with opulent furnishings. The downstairs Polo Club and Club X areas pack out on weekends, when bouncers can be strict; just the main bars open on other nights. One of them, the Riding Room, has cabaret shows. (📞0845 659 5905; www.pologlasgow.co.uk; 84 Wilson St; admission £3-7; ⏰9pm-3am)

Spiritualist
COCKTAIL BAR

28 🚇 MAP P88, D3

This former library still features lofty shelving but these days it's craft gins and spirits that they bear. The noble, high-ceilinged interior of this upmarket bar is stunningly attractive, and it's a great place for an evening cocktail or gin and tonic, with a huge range to choose from. It also does food. (📞0141-248 4165; www.thespiritualistglasgow.com; 62 Miller St; ⏰noon-11pm Sun-Thu, to midnight Fri & Sat; 📶)

Entertainment

Old Fruitmarket
CONCERT VENUE

29 ⭐ MAP P88, G3

In central Merchant City, this former market, a spectacular vaulted space, has concerts, both classical and rock. (📞0141-353 8000; www. glasgowconcerthalls.com; Candleriggs)

City Halls

CONCERT VENUE

30 ⭐ MAP P88, G3

In the heart of Merchant City, there are regular performances in this beautiful rectangular auditorium by the Scottish Chamber Orchestra and the Scottish Symphony Orchestra. (✆0141-353 8000; www.glasgowconcerthalls.com; Candleriggs)

13th Note Café

LIVE MUSIC

31 ⭐ MAP P88, F5

Cosy basement venue with small independent bands as well as weekend DJs and regular comedy and theatre performances. At street level the pleasant cafe does decent vegetarian and vegan food (£7 to £10, until 9pm). (✆0141-553 1638; www.13thnote.co.uk; 50-60 King St; ⏰noon-11pm or midnight; 🛜)

Tron Theatre

THEATRE

32 ⭐ MAP P88, F4

Tron Theatre, located in the James Adam–designed Tron Kirk, fronted by an elaborate bell tower, stages contemporary Scottish and international performances. There's also a good cafe-bar-restaurant at the back. Enter via Chisholm St. (✆0141-552 4267; www.tron.co.uk; 63 Trongate)

Riding Room

CABARET

33 ⭐ MAP P88, D3

Plenty of fun and strong cocktails served in weird receptacles at

---

Local Experiences 👍

Quirky boozers Pubs that go for character over turnover include **Babbity Bowster** (p95) and **Rab Ha's** (Map p88, E3; ✆0141-370 8818; www.rabhas.co.uk; 83 Hutcheson St; r £90-110).

Lunch breaks People pop out of work to places like **Picnic** (p91) for a quick, quality lunch that won't break the bank.

Offbeat shops Away from the Style Mile, locals cruise shops like **Mr Ben** and **Record Fayre** (p98) for second-hand bargains.

---

this nightly cabaret and burlesque venue. Expect plenty of sauce here in the heart of the Pink Triangle. Cosy booths have the best seats and can be prebooked online. (✆0845 659 5904; www.theridingroom.co.uk; 58 Virginia St; ⏰9pm-3am Sun-Thu, from 7pm Fri & Sat)

Shopping

Mr Ben

CLOTHING

34 🔒 MAP P88, F5

This cute place is one of Glasgow's best destinations for vintage clothing, with a great selection of brands like Fred Perry, as well as more glam choices and even outdoor gear. (✆0141-553 1936; www.mrbenretroclothing.com; 101 King St;

⏱12.30-6pm Mon & Tue, from 10.30am Wed-Sat, 12.30-5.30pm Sun)

Argyll Arcade
JEWELLERY

35 🔒 MAP P88, B3

This splendid historic arcade doglegs between Buchanan and Argyle Sts and has done since before Victoria reigned. It's quite a sight with its end-to-end jewellery and watch shops. Top-hatted door-people greet nervously excited couples shopping for diamond rings. (📞0141-248 5257; www.argyll-arcade.com; Buchanan St; ⏱10am-5.30pm Mon-Sat, noon-5pm Sun)

Princes Square
SHOPPING CENTRE

36 🔒 MAP P88, B3

Set in a magnificent 1841 renovated square with elaborate ironwork and an exuberant metal leaf-and-peacock facade, this place has lots of beauty and fashion outlets, including Vivienne Westwood. There's a good selection of restaurants and cafes, as well as a bar with a roof terrace. (📞0141-221 0324; www.princessquare.co.uk; 48 Buchanan St; ⏱10am-7pm Mon-Fri, 9am-6pm Sat, 11am-5pm Sun)

Glasgow Print Studio
ART

37 🔒 MAP P88, F5

There are always high-quality exhibitions and prints displayed at this well laid-out gallery. There's an entrance on King St. (📞0141-552 0704; www.glasgowprintstudio.co.uk;

103 Trongate; ⏱10am-5.30pm Tue-Sat, noon-5pm Sun)

Monorail
MUSIC

This indie record shop has a care-fully curated selection of alternative and experimental rock, punk, reggae, soul and jazz. It shares space with Mono (p91; see 9 ✖ Map p88, F5), a vegan cafe, so you can browse while your food is prepared. (📞0141-552 9458; www.monorailmusic.com; Kings Ct, 95 King St; ⏱11am-7pm Mon-Sat, from noon Sun)

Luke & Jack
ADULT

38 🔒 MAP P88, D3

With very friendly staff and a range of saucy items that you might not want your mother to see, this is a favourite with the gay community – it's in Pink Triangle central – but there's plenty here for everyone, from humorous novelties to fetish gear. The basement gallery in the same building is worth checking out too. (📞0141-552 5699; www.lukeandjack.co.uk; 45 Virginia St; ⏱11am-6pm Mon-Thu, 10.30am-6.30pm Fri & Sat, noon-5pm Sun)

Record Fayre
MUSIC

39 🔒 MAP P88, F5

This back-to-basics music shop has been around for years and is worth checking out for its well-priced second-hand vinyl. (📞0141-552 5696; www.recordfayre.co.uk; 13 Chisholm St; ⏱9am-5pm Mon-Sat, from 10am Sun)

TREASUREGALORE/SHUTTERSTOCK ©

Princes Square

Merchant Square Craft & Design Fair

MARKET

40 🔒 MAP P88, G3

This weekend market fills the Merchant Sq space with stalls peddling handmade crafts, from candles to jewellery to paintings. Nearly all are made locally in Glasgow. (📞0141-552 3038; www.merchantsquareglasgow.com; Merchant Sq, Candleriggs; 🕙11am-6pm Sat, from noon Sun)

St Enoch Centre

SHOPPING CENTRE

41 🔒 MAP P88, C4

This sizeable, ugly glass-roofed centre bookends the southern boundary of Glasgow's shopping mile. Among its many shops is a branch of Hamley's, the historic London toy store. (📞0141-204 3900; www.st-enoch.com; St Enoch Sq; 🕙9am-7pm Mon-Fri, to 6pm Sat, 10am-6pm Sun, some shops close an hour later Thu & Sat; 🛜)

Street Level Photoworks

PHOTOGRAPHY

42 🔒 MAP P88, F5

Fine photography exhibitions are allied with a program of courses and workshops here. There's also an entrance on King St. (📞0141-552 2151; www.streetlevelphotoworks.org; 103 Trongate; 🕙10am-5pm Tue-Sat, from noon Sun)

Explore ◉

Southside & the Clyde

Once a thriving shipbuilding area, the Clyde sank into dereliction post-war but has been subject to extensive rejuvenation. Beyond it, the Southside is a busy web of roads dotted with sizeable parks. It's an intriguingly multicultural part of Glasgow, with an up-and-coming food scene and thriving cultural centres; excellent attractions are also dotted across it.

The two principal attractions on the Clyde, the Riverside Museum (p102) and the Glasgow Science Centre (p104), are family-friendly affairs that could absorb children (and adults) for several hours each, particularly the latter. It's under a mile's walk between them via the Clydeside Distillery (p108).

The Southside's attractions, several of which are architecturally notable buildings, are widely spread out, so time planning your route will be well spent. Some attractions are accessible via the subway; others are better reached by train or bus. The famous Burrell Collection (p108) is due to reopen in 2022; aim to spend at least half a day there.

Getting There & Around

🚌 The bus is the most useful way to reach many places in the south and along the river.

Ⓢ Half of the circular subway network runs south of the Clyde, with seven Southside stops.

🚃 Trains can be handy for reaching certain attractions.

Southside Map on p106

Tall Ship outside the Riverside Museum (p102) EQROY/SHUTTERSTOCK ©

Top Experience 📷

Explore a Tall Ship at Riverside Museum

Glasgow's most visited attraction is an entertaining museum of transport set in a vibrant modern building on the banks of the Clyde. Its substantial interior holds every conceivable variety of vehicle from locomotives to bicycles; kids are in heaven here as they explore the variety. Outside, the beautiful three-masted Tall Ship provides another thrill.

◉ MAP P106, A1

☏ 0141-287 2720

www.glasgowmuseums.com

100 Pointhouse Pl

admission free

🕙 10am-5pm Mon-Thu & Sat, from 11am Fri & Sun

The Building

Set on the site of one of Glasgow's most prominent former shipyards, A & J Inglis, the striking museum was designed by Zaha Hadid. The front and back facades have enormous visual impact, with the building's zinc cladding zigzagging across the top of vast dark glass windows.

Main Street

This recreated cobbled street is an atmospheric display of shops as they would have appeared in the late 19th and early 20th centuries. Pop in to admire the saddler, pawnbrokers, portrait photographer and more. There's a pub, too, of course.

Wall of Cars

Three levels of motor vehicles are dramatically displayed on one wall of the museum. This 'Wall of Cars' highlights Scottish-made vehicles, such as the iconic Hillman Imp. While it's certainly a spectacular way to display them, you don't get a very good look at the topmost ones. There's a similar wall of motorcycles at the other end of the museum.

Ship Conveyor

The small, meandering upstairs floor can be a welcome retreat from the downstairs hubbub. The key sight up here is the Ship Conveyor, where beautiful models of famous ships built along the Clyde sail gracefully past your eyes.

Tall Ship

Docked outside the museum, the elegant three-masted sailing ship, *Glenlee,* was built on the Clyde and launched in 1896. On board are three decks to explore, with family-friendly displays about the ship's history, restoration and shipboard life during its heyday. Upkeep costs are high, so consider buying the guidebook or having a coffee below decks.

★ Top Tips

o The museum fills with families at weekends; visit on a weekday if you can, though school groups can also be noisy.

o The Tall Ship opens daily at 10am, so you can visit it before the museum opens on Fridays and Sundays.

o There's a pleasant riverside path linking the Riverside Museum and the Kelvingrove Art Gallery & Museum.

✕ Take a Break

The museum and Tall Ship both have a cafe but there are no other eateries in easy reach.

Ice-cream and other kiosks are open outside the museum at weekends.

Top Experience 📷

Get Interactive at Glasgow Science Centre

This undervisited science museum on the banks of the Clyde is a real delight. It's packed full of brilliantly interactive displays and exhibits about all areas of science and is huge fun for all ages; you could easily spend most of a day here discovering everything there is to see and do.

◎ MAP P106, B2

www.glasgowscience
centre.org
50 Pacific Quay
adult/child £12/10, IMAX,
Glasgow Tower or Plan-
etarium extra £2.50-3.50
🕐 10am-5pm daily Apr-
Oct, to 3pm Wed-Fri, to
5pm Sat & Sun Nov-Mar

Planetarium

On the 1st floor and accessed with an additional ticket, this excellent facility has three different shows suitable for various ages. Even if you don't see a show, hit the space exhibition in the foyer for good up-to-date astronomical information.

Question of Perception

On the 1st floor, this could be called Question of Deception as all your senses are deceived by the interactive exhibits. There are some great illusions here; all ages will find something to delight or flummox them here.

Powering the Future

On the 2nd floor, this display looks at energy consumption (with some sobering statistics) and how the world might be powered in the future, with in-depth information on a range of technologies. Highlights include making some tough policy decisions in the energy minister simulation, racing cars or hitting the energy dance floor.

Bodyworks

On the museum's top floor, this all-ages display has good, detailed information about the human body and modern medicine. You are bound to discover something that you didn't know, but there's plenty of fun to be had here too, with numerous interactive displays. Test your grip strength and compare yourself to other visitors, or try out your surgical skills.

Glasgow Tower

An additional or separate ticket lets you up this high-tech rotating tower, which offers the best views in town from its 127m height; it offers a terrific perspective of the Clyde and across the city. Tablets in the viewing cabin let you zoom in on what you are looking at, while an exhibition on the city is at ground level. It closes when winds are high.

★ Top Tips

o There's an IMAX cinema here too; check the session times for this and the planetarium ahead of your visit.

o The museum can get very busy midweek with school groups, but it's big enough for you to find free exhibits somewhere in the complex.

✗ Take a Break

There's a cafe in the museum, plus an additional one at weekends, as well as a Starbucks in the IMAX cinema.

Outside on the quay, a little food truck, the Cabin, does high-quality coffee, home baking and lunches.

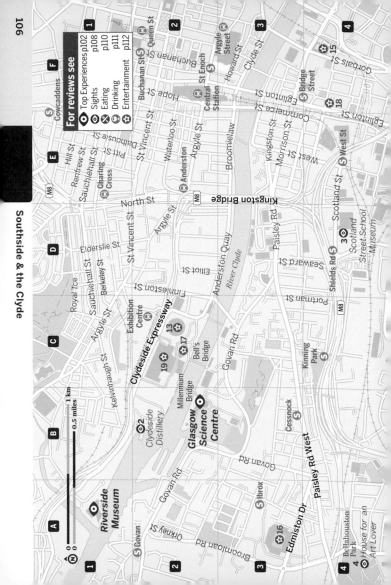

Southside & the Clyde

Cathcart Rd

Aikenhead Rd

Cathcart Rd

Calder St

Crosshill

Dixon Ave

Pollokshaws Rd

Hidden Gardens

7

14

9

12

Pollokshields East

Queens Park

Queens Dr

Queens Dr

Queens Park

6

Prospecthill Rd

Scottish Football Museum 5

Hampden Park

Battlefield Rd

Langside Rd

Langside Rd

Langside Ave

Longside Ave

Pollokshaws Rd

St Andrew's Dr

Albert Dr

Nithsdale Rd

Pollokshields West

Darnley Rd

Pollokshields West

Crossmyloof

10

11

8

Kilmarnock Rd

Pollokshaws Rd

Albert Dr

St Andrew's Dr

Titwood Rd

Haggs Rd

Sherbrooke Ave

Dumbreck

Nithsdale Rd

Maxwell Dr

Dumbreck Rd

Dumbreck Rd

Burrell Collection 1

Pollok Ave

F

E

D

C

B

A

5

6

7

8

Sights

Burrell Collection
GALLERY

1 MAP P106, A7

One of Glasgow's top attractions, this outstanding museum 3 miles out of town houses everything from Chinese porcelain and medieval furniture to paintings by Cézanne. The tapestry collection is a particular highlight. It's closed for refurbishment, and is due to reopen in 2022. The new building will have double the exhibition space as well as a cafe. Meanwhile, some items are on display at the Kelvingrove Art Gallery & Museum (p116). (☑0141-287 2550; www.glasgowlife.org.uk; Pollok Country Park; admission free; ☺closed)

The Clyde

Previously renowned as one of the world's great shipbuilding zones, Glasgow's river was left forlorn after the industry declined. While there's work still to be done, parts of the Clyde have had a dramatic facelift and it's now studded with significant architectural elements, attracting concert-goers and museum visitors to its banks. The **Clyde Walk-way** (Map p106, F3) runs right through the city centre and upstream as far as Lanark; it's a good way to appreciate Glasgow's major artery.

Clydeside Distillery
DISTILLERY

2 MAP P106, B2

It's great to see this old pumphouse by the Clyde being put to good use as a malt whisky distillery run by proper whisky folk. It's an impressive set-up, with the stills overlooking the river (don't worry, the water comes from Loch Katrine, not the Clyde). The tour (1¼ hours) is engaging, with some history of the Clyde. It includes a tasting of three malts. (☑0141-212 1401; www.theclydeside.com; The Pumphouse, 100 Stobcross Rd; tour adult/child £15/5; ☺10am-4pm Sep-Jun, to 4.30pm Jul & Aug)

Scotland Street School Museum
NOTABLE BUILDING

3 MAP P106, D4

Mackintosh's Scotland Street School seems a bit forlorn these days, on a windswept industrial street with no babble of young voices filling its corridors. Nevertheless, it's worth a visit for its stunning facade and the interesting museum of education that occupies the interior. Reconstructions of classrooms from various points in the school's lifetime, combined with grumbling headmaster and cleaner, will have older visitors recalling their own schooldays. It's right opposite Shields Road subway station and there's also an OK cafe. (☑0141-287 0504; www.glasgowlife.org.uk; 225 Scotland St; admission free; ☺10am-5pm Tue-Thu & Sat, from 11am Fri & Sun)

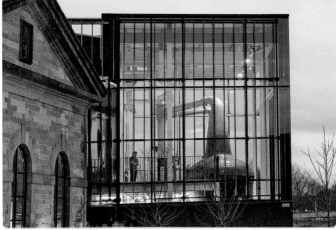
IAIN MASTERTON/ALAMY STOCK PHOTO ©

Clydeside Distillery

House for an Art Lover
NOTABLE BUILDING

4 ◉ MAP P106, A4

Although designed in 1901 as an entry in a competition run by a German magazine, this house in Bellahouston Park was not built until the 1990s. Mackintosh worked closely with his wife on the design and her influence is evident, especially in the rose motif. The overall effect of this brilliant architect's ideas is one of space and light. Buses 9, 10 and 38 all run here from downtown; check the website for opening hours, as it's regularly booked for events. (📞0141-353 4770; www.houseforan artlover.co.uk; Bellahouston Park, Dumbreck Rd; adult/child £6/4.50;

🕐check online, roughly 10am-4pm Mon-Fri, to noon Sat, to 2pm Sun)

Scottish Football Museum
MUSEUM

5 ◉ MAP P106, F8

At Hampden Park, the national stadium, this museum covers the history of the game in Scotland and the considerable influence of Scots on the world game. It's crammed full of impressive memorabilia, including a cap and match ticket from the very first international football game ever played, held in Glasgow in 1872. You can also take a tour of the stadium (adult/child £8/3.50; combined ticket with museum £13/5), home ground to both Scotland and lower division outfit Queens Park. (The Hampden Experience; 📞0141-616

6139; www.scottishfootballmuseum.org.uk; Hampden Park; adult/child £8/3; ◷10am-5pm Mon-Sat, from 11am Sun)

Queens Park
PARK

6 ◉ MAP P106, E7

This Southside landmark was laid out in Victorian times as the city expanded; it's still a major community focus. Kids attempt to feed the ducks, who try to hold their own against the bullying gulls. Elsewhere, there's a glasshouse and pleasant views atop the hill. (Pollokshaws Rd)

Hidden Gardens
GARDENS

7 ◉ MAP P106, E6

Out the back of the Tramway (p112) performance space, this pretty garden has works of art but also functions as a multicultural community space. (☏0141-433 2722; www.thehiddengardens.org.uk; 25a Albert Dr; admission free; ◷10am-8pm Tue-Sat, noon-6pm Sun Apr-Sep, 10am-4pm Tue-Sat, noon-4pm Sun Oct-Mar)

Eating

Cafe Strange Brew
CAFE **$**

8 ⊗ MAP P106, C7

This has such cachet as the Southside's, if not the city's, best cafe, that you'll be waiting in line most days. It's worth the enforced contemplation though, with generous, vibrant, filling brunchy fare that draws on global influences as well as closer-to-

House for an Art Lover (p109)

CORNFIELD/SHUTTERSTOCK ©

home inspiration. Presentation is a high point; leave room for the sinfully sticky desserts. (☎0141-440 7290; www.facebook.com/cafestrangebrew, 1082 Pollokshaws Rd; dishes £5-11; ⏰9am-5pm Mon-Sat, to 4pm Sun)

Ranjit's Kitchen INDIAN $

9 ⓂMAP P106, E6

A Sikh family brings authentic home-cooked flavours from the Punjab to this sweet little Southside spot, whose elongated wooden tables soon pack out with diners. Daily dhal and sabji specials are reliably delicious but it's all tasty and excellent value. No alcohol. (☎0141-423 8222; www.ranjitskitchen.com; 607 Pollokshaws Rd; dishes £4-6; ⏰noon-8.30pm Tue-Sun; 🔧)

Drinking

Glad Cafe CAFE

10 ⓂMAP P106, D7

This social enterprise cafe and venue incorporates a thrift shop and coworking space. But don't just come for the cause; it's a cracking spot in its own right, with solid wooden furniture, excellent coffee, craft beers, interesting food and a laid-back bohemian vibe that makes it a perfect escape. Check the website for upcoming events, which range from bands to comedy. (☎0141-636 6119; www.thegladcafe.co.uk; 1006 Pollokshaws Rd; ⏰9am-11pm Mon-Wed, to midnight Thu & Fri, 10am-midnight Sat, 10am-11pm Sun; 🛜)

Butterfly and the Pig Southside PUB

11 ⓂMAP P106, D7

The southern incarnation of this well-loved Bath St bar occupies an extravagantly decorated traditional pub opposite Queens Park. It's a laid-back, pleasingly louche spot to kick back with a drink or try to decipher the whimsical food menu. (📞0141-632 5230; www.thebutterfly andthepig.com; 1041 Pollokshaws Rd; 🕐11am-midnight Mon-Sat, from noon Sun; 🛜)

Rum Shack

BAR

12 🚍 MAP P106, E6

Near Queens Park station, this upbeat spot doles out more than a hundred varieties of rum. It backs up the Caribbean theme with Jamaican and Creole-influenced dishes, and regular live reggae and ska in the adjacent venue. (📞0141-237 4432; www.rumshackglasgow.com; 657 Pollokshaws Rd; 🕐11am-midnight; 🛜)

Entertainment

Hydro

LIVE PERFORMANCE

13 ⭐ MAP P106, C2

A spectacular modern building to keep the adjacent 'Armadillo' (p112) company, the Hydro amphitheatre is a phenomenally popular venue for big-name concerts and shows. (📞0844 395 4000; www.thessehydro.com; Finnieston Quay; 🛜)

Tramway

PERFORMING ARTS

14 ⭐ MAP P106, E6

Occupying a former tram depot, this buzzy cultural centre has performance and exhibition spaces as well as a popular cafe. It's a real Southside community hub, with an unusual garden (p110) out the back. It attracts cutting-edge theatrical groups, is the home of Scottish Ballet and hosts a varied range of artistic exhibitions. It's very close to Pollokshields East train station. (📞0845 330 3501; www.tramway.org; 25 Albert Dr; 🕐9.30am-8pm Mon-Sat, 10am-6pm Sun; 🛜)

Citizens' Theatre

THEATRE

15 ⭐ MAP P106, F4

South of the Clyde, this is one of the top theatres in Scotland. It's well worth trying to catch a performance here. The building has enjoyed a recent major redevelopment. (📞0141-429 0022; www.citz.co.uk; 119 Gorbals St)

Rangers FC

FOOTBALL

16 ⭐ MAP P106, A3

One of Glasgow's big two football clubs, Rangers play in blue and traditionally represent the Protestant, pro-Union side of the divide. They returned to the top division in 2016 after a financial meltdown in 2012. Tours of the stadium and trophy room run Friday to Sunday (£15/5 per adult/child). Take the subway to Ibrox station. (📞0871 702 1972; www.rangers.co.uk; Ibrox Stadium, 150 Edmiston Dr)

Clyde Auditorium

LIVE PERFORMANCE

17 ⭐ MAP P106, C2

Also known as the Armadillo because of its bizarre shape, the

DAVID MCELROY/SHUTTERSTOCK ©

Queens Park (p110)

Clyde adjoins the SEC Centre auditorium, and caters for big national and international acts. (☎0844 395 4000; www.sec.co.uk; Finnieston Quay)

Academy Glasgow CONCERT VENUE

18 ⭐ MAP P106, F4

This former cinema in the Gorbals district is a bit forlorn now without much around, but it's a key venue for big-name touring acts, with a 2500-seat capacity. Bus 3 stops here; it's also very close to Bridge Street subway station. (O₂Academy; ☎0141-332 2232; www.academymusic group.com; 121 Eglinton St)

SEC Centre LIVE PERFORMANCE

19 ⭐ MAP P106, C2

The headquarters of the complex that includes the Clyde Auditorium and Hydro is an exhibition space and sometime concert venue. (☎0844 395 4000; www.sec.co.uk; Finnieston Quay)

Explore ⊕
West End

With its appealing student buzz, modish bars and cafes and bohemian swagger, the West End is for many the most engaging area of Glasgow. Streets of elegant terraced houses and ample parkland cover large areas of the district, centred around the Victorian grandeur of the University of Glasgow and Kelvingrove Art Gallery & Museum. Glasgow's key eat streets are also here.

Key sights are fairly close together in this neighbourhood's centre. Kelvingrove Art Gallery & Museum (p116) could easily take half a day or more to explore, while Hunterian Museum (p121) and art gallery (p121), incorporating Mackintosh House, are also worth plenty of time. But much of the pleasure of the district is in wandering, whether it's browsing shops down Byres Rd, pacing the River Kelvin path, or strolling the Botanic Gardens (p128). Dedicate at least two evenings of your stay in Glasgow to the West End: one around Great Western and Byres Rds, the other on the Finnieston strip of eateries on Argyle St.

Getting There & Around

🚌 From the city centre, buses 9, 16 and 23 run towards Kelvingrove; buses 8, 11 and 16 to the University of Glasgow; and buses 20, 44 and 66 to Byres Rd (among others).

S Head to Kelvinbridge station for Great Western Rd, Hillhead for Byres Rd, and Kelvinhall for the university and Kelvingrove Art Gallery & Museum.

West End Map on p126

Vodka Wodka, Ashton Lane (p138) LOU ARMOR/SHUTTERSTOCK ©

Top Experience 📷

Hear an Organ Recital at Kelvingrove Art Gallery & Museum

Built in the grand style at the time of collectors, colonies and world exhibitions, this red sandstone Victorian museum covers a huge range of subjects from archaeology to natural history in an accessible modern way. Its art collection is a particular standout, with key Scottish movements well represented alongside some fine European masterpieces.

⊙ MAP P126, C5

📞 0141-276 9599

www.glasgowmuseums.com

Argyle St

admission free

🕙 10am-5pm Mon-Thu & Sat, from 11am Fri & Sun

First Impressions

There are over a million objects in the museum's collection, but fortunately they've pared things down, so you won't feel overwhelmed. Enter from either side after admiring the exterior; the streetside facade is less grand than the one at the back because it was opened as part of an international exhibition centred on Kelvingrove Park.

Next, take a while to appreciate the building's interior, with its high central hall, elaborate lamps and impressive organ (recitals at 1pm).

The museum is divided into two wings, one focusing on Life (history, archaeology and natural history) and the other on Expression (art).

First Floor: Expression

Start with the art. Upstairs in the hall you'll find a mass of hanging heads, a striking installation by Sophie Cave. The Dutch gallery has some quality pieces, including Rembrandt's magnificent *A Man in Armour,* employing chiaroscuro techniques learned from Caravaggio.

The next-but-one French gallery holds a fine Renoir portrait of his pupil Valentine Fray, and an early Van Gogh depicting his Glaswegian flatmate Alexander Reid. Monet's *Vétheuil* offers a quintessential representation of both impressionism and the French countryside, contrast it with the less ethereal landscape by Cézanne located alongside it. One of Dufy's famous canvases, *The Jetty at Trouville-Deauville,* also hangs in this room, as do works by many other masters.

The Scottish landscape gallery has some jaw-dropping depictions of Highland scenes. Standing in front of Gustave Doré's *Glen Massan,* you can almost feel the drizzle and smell the heather. David Wilkie's *The Cottar's Saturday Night* is based on the poem by Robert Burns, which you can listen to alongside it.

★ Top Tips

o There are free guided tours daily at 11am and 2.30pm plus an organ recital at 1pm.

o In the central atrium, the Mini Museum is aimed at kids aged under five.

o Nearly every object here has an interpretive paragraph; it's a great spot to learn about art.

✗ Take a Break

The museum has a pleasant cafe in the atrium; head across the road to Brewdog Glasgow (p136) for a fine range of craft beers.

Butchershop Bar & Grill (p134) is right opposite the museum; chow down on its tasty aged steaks.

While you're up here, don't miss the paintings around the arcade, or the small gallery devoted to the Scottish Colourists, four artists working in the early decades of the 20th century who brought a French flourish of colour and light to the Scottish art scene.

A Dalí Masterwork

Arguably the highlight of the whole museum hangs in a small 1st-floor room near the central atrium. Based on dreams, Salvador Dalí's *Christ of St John of the Cross* is perhaps his greatest work. Forget ridiculous moustaches and surrealist frippery: this is a serious, awesomely powerful painting. A sinewy crucified man-god looks down through an infinity of sky and darkness to a simple fishing boat in Galilee (or Catalunya in this case). The artist was interested in science and associates the nucleus of the atom with Christ here after a 'cosmic dream' he had. He strapped a Hollywood stuntman to a gantry to get the musculature right.

Ground Floor: Expression

Downstairs, check out the rooms Looking at Art and the Art Discovery Centre, partly aimed at kids but well worth a stroll, then head for the large room devoted to the Glasgow Boys. Inspired by Whistler, these artists broke with romanticism to pioneer a more modern style. Compare William Kennedy's grounded *Stirling Station* or the realism of James Guthrie's *A Funeral Service in the Highlands* with those misty Scottish landscapes upstairs. Also noteworthy in this space are John Lavery's famous theatrical portrait of Anna Pavlova, and EA Hornel's much-reproduced *The Coming of Spring,* one of several of his works that feature young girls in a seasonal landscape.

You will have seen most of the paintings now, but there's plenty left to discover if you're not worn out. Try the room dedicated to art deco and Glasgow Style interiors and designs. 'Margaret has genius, I have only talent', said Charles Rennie Mackintosh of his wife, and there's a good display of her work here – particularly her exquisite gesso panels – as well as that of her sister, Frances Macdonald.

Western Side: Life

The other side of the museum, dominated by a hanging Spitfire, has two floors of rooms featuring impressive prehistoric and Viking-era carved stones, Egyptian grave goods and other archaeological finds. Suits of armour are cleverly placed in an exhibition about the human consequences of war, and there are some fine social history displays. The taxidermied animals downstairs are a reminder of the museum's Victorian past; Sir Roger the elephant is a notable Glasgow character in his day. Don't miss John Fulton's elaborate orrery, a working model of the solar system.

Top Experience 📷

Marvel at the Victorian University of Glasgow

First founded in the sacristy of Glasgow Cathedral, then long occupying city-centre premises, Glasgow's foremost university moved out west in Victorian times. As well as the impressive main university building, an excellent museum and art gallery are located here, along with a recreation of the exquisite house of Charles Rennie Mackintosh and his wife, Margaret Macdonald.

◎ MAP P126, C3

📞 0141-330 1835

www.gla.ac.uk

University Ave

Hunterian Museum

Housed in the sandstone main university building, this quirky **museum** (☎0141-330 4221; www.hunterian.gla.ac.uk; University Ave; admission free; ☺10am-5pm Tue-Sat, 11am-4pm Sun) contains the collection of renowned one-time student, William Hunter (1718–83). Pickled organs in glass jars take their place alongside geological phenomena, potsherds gleaned from ancient brochs, dinosaur skeletons and a creepy case of deformed animals. The main halls of the exhibition, with their high vaulted roofs, are magnificent in themselves.

Hunterian Art Gallery

North of the main building, on the other side of University Ave, this **art gallery** (☎0141-330 4221; www.hunterian.gla.ac.uk; 82 Hillhead St; admission free; ☺10am-5pm Tue-Sat, 11am-4pm Sun) houses another part of Hunter's collection as well as later acquisitions by the university. A good selection of Flemish old masters is followed by an in-depth look at Whistler and the Aesthetic movement. A highlight is Whistler's peacock cartoon for a mural in the home of a patron, with a dig at his employer. Paintings by Whistler's protégés, the Glasgow Boys, and works by the Scottish Colourists are usually on display.

Mackintosh House

Attached to the Hunterian Art Gallery, this extraordinary **house** (☎0141-330 4221; www.hunterian.gla.ac.uk; 82 Hillhead St; adult/child £6/3; ☺10am-5pm Tue-Sat, 11am-4pm Sun) is a reassembled replica of the dwelling of Charles Rennie Mackintosh and Margaret Macdonald, which stood nearby. Stunning interiors in harmonious schemes of white, beige and grey offer luminosity and a stage for the marvellous furniture on display. Look out for the heart and bird shapes typical of the Glasgow Style, the high-backed chairs, exquisite dressers and the perfect white drawing room. Visits are by guided tour in the morning and self-guided in the afternoon.

★ Top Tips

o Visits to the Mackintosh House are guided in the morning and self-guided in the afternoon, so pick according to your preference.

o A large new exhibition space is gradually being developed at Kelvin Hall. It's likely that some or all of these university collections will move into it, but not until 2023 or so.

✖ Take a Break

Between a visit to the museum and the gallery, stroll down University Ave for lunch at the inventive and reliable bistro Stravaigin (p130) on Gibson St.

It's a short walk to the wall-to-wall bars and restaurants of cute little Ashton Lane; we recommend Brel (p136) for a drink in the beer garden.

West End Marvel at the Victorian University of Glasgow

Walking Tour 🥾

A Day in the West End

While you certainly might want a busy sightseeing day to tick off the area's museums, it's nice to take it slowly and soak up the laid-back bohemian vibe of the West End. You can spend a happy time browsing the district's small shops, strolling the lovely parks, and trying out the myriad bars and numerous quality eating options.

Walk Facts

Start Byres Road;
S Hillhead

End Ashton Lane;
S Hillhead

Length 4km; 3 hours

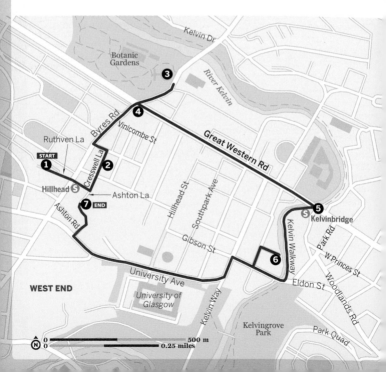

❶ Ruthven Lane

Head across the road from the subway to this complex of laneway businesses. There's not much glitz; the shops are all pretty authentic and unglamorous, with some retro gems ready for discovery in places like **Antiques & Interiors** (p141). There are a couple of fine places to eat here too.

❷ De Courcy's Arcade

Cross Byres Rd to find this tiny backstreet **shopping arcade** (p140) where you can browse bijou outlets of substantial charm. There's new and vintage clothing, art, homewares and more on offer here. It's a good spot to find an out-of-the-ordinary gift for somebody back home. Hungry or thirsty? Drop by nearby Ashton Lane, which is wall-to-wall with bars, restaurants and cafes.

❸ Ferns & More

The jewel of the West End's lovely Botanic Gardens is the **Kibble Palace** (p128), a beautifully restored Victorian glasshouse that is home to a fine collection of tree ferns. There's a tearoom nearby, but picking up a picnic from the delis on Byres Rd is definitely the way to go if the weather is clement.

❹ Lunchtime Theatre

The converted church Òran Mór is the venue for **A Play, a Pie and a Pint** (p138), an innovative lunchtime theatre session in the pub. Your ticket includes the pie (vegetarian option available) and a drink. Check the website to see what's on; expect irreverence.

❺ Along the Kelvin

Head along Great Western Rd, browsing the shops as you pass, then drop down to the lovely **riverside path** that runs along the Kelvin. It makes a lovely escape from the urban bustle around.

❻ Time for a Cuppa

Near the river, tucked-away **Tchai Ovna** (p137) is a cosy den stocking around a hundred different teas and infusions. It makes a fine spot to while away an hour or two and feel the local boho vibe.

❼ Catch a Film

Back on Ashton Lane, things get busy in the evening. Locals love the **Grosvenor Cinema** (p138) here. Drop in, catch a film, then discuss it over a beer or a meal in the surrounding bars.

Walking Tour 🚶‍♂️

West End Walk

This walk is a highlights tour of the western part of Glasgow, taking in the key shopping and eating strips as well as parks, pubs, the university and the major sights. It could be a brisk stroll to get your bearings before returning in depth, or a lazy meander browsing boutiques, museums and restaurants that could easily occupy a day.

Walk Facts

Start Kelvinbridge subway station

End Argyle St, Finnieston

Length 3 miles; 2 hours

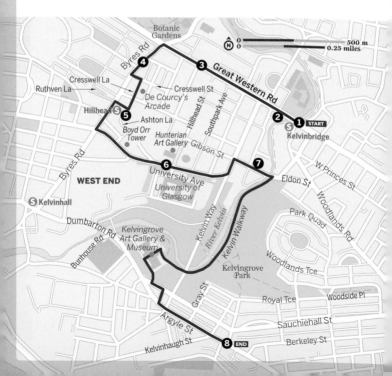

❶ Kelvinbridge

Emerge from the subway and turn left across **Great Western Bridge (Kelvinbridge)**, emblazoned with the lion rampant of the Hillhead burgh on the south side and the city coat of arms on the north. It crosses the leafy course of the Kelvin, a tributary of the Clyde.

❷ A Riverside Tavern

Below the bridge, note the riverside bar **Inn Deep** (p135), a fine place for a drink. It might be a bit early for one, but it's a spot to come back to. The coat of arms alongside the entrance is that of the Caledonian Railway Company; there was formerly a station here.

❸ Great Western Road

Continue along Great Western Rd, stopping for a browse in **Glasgow Vintage Company** (p138) and **Caledonia Books** (p140). At the corner of Byres Rd, a former church is now **Oràn Mór** (p136); consider its lunchtime theatre session **A Play, a Pie and a Pint** (p138). Across the road stretches the **Botanic Gardens** (p128).

❹ Byres Road

Turn left down Byres Rd, investigating the interesting shops on the left in this first section. At Cresswell St, turn left and then right down Cresswell Lane to check out tiny **De Courcy's Arcade** (p140).

❺ Laneways

Continuing down this lane brings you to the bar-heavy Ashton Lane, where **Ubiquitous Chip** (p134) is still one of Scotland's best places to eat. Turn right opposite Jinty McGuinty's to reach Byres Rd again. Cross and examine the quirky shops down Ruthven Lane, accessed directly opposite.

❻ University Avenue

Back on Byres Rd, head south, then turn left up University Ave. The ugly 1960s **Boyd Orr tower** is soon replaced by more typical sandstone terraces as you climb the hill. On the left is the **Hunterian Art Gallery** (p121) and **Mackintosh House** (p121); on the right, wander through the quadrangles of the University of Glasgow's main building, home to the **Hunterian Museum** (p121).

❼ To the Kelvin

At the bottom of University Ave, turn left, then right onto Gibson St, home to quality lunch stops like **Stravaigin** (p130). Cross the bridge and turn right into the park, bearing right down to the river and the **Kelvin Walkway**.

❽ Kelvingrove

Follow the walkway for half a mile through lovely Kelvingrove Park to reach the **Kelvingrove Art Gallery & Museum** (p116). From here it's a short hop to the Finnieston eating strip on Argyle St.

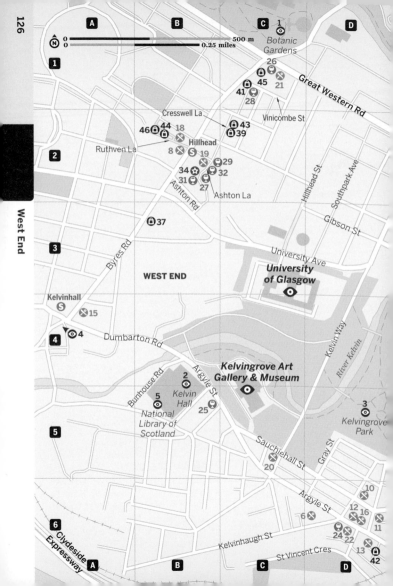

West End

N

0   500 m
0   0.25 miles

A   B   C   D

1

Botanic Gardens

26

45

21

Great Western Rd

41

28

Cresswell La

43

Vinicombe St

46   44   18

39

Ruthven La

8

Hillhead

19

29

34

32

31

27

Ashton La

Ashton Rd

37

2

WEST END

Byres Rd

University Ave

University of Glasgow

Hillhead St

Southpark Ave

Gibson St

3

Kelvinhall

15

4

Dumbarton Rd

Kelvingrove Art Gallery & Museum

Kelvin Way

River Kelvin

Bunhouse Rd

2

Kelvin Hall

Argyle St

5

National Library of Scotland

25

3

Kelvingrove Park

Gray St

Sauchiehall St

20

Argyle St

10

6

12   16

11

24   22

13

42

Clydeside Expressway

Kelvinhaugh St

St Vincent Cres

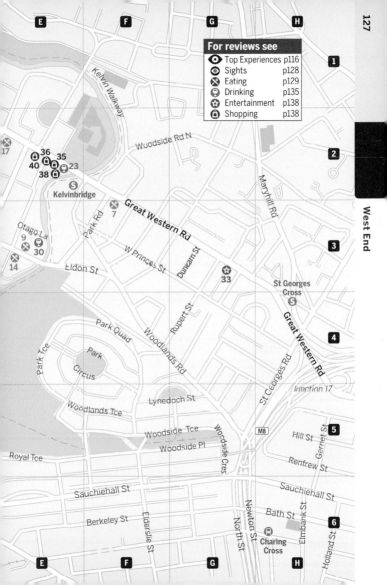

West End

For reviews see

◉	Top Experiences	p116
◉	Sights	p128
✖	Eating	p129
☻	Drinking	p135
★	Entertainment	p138
🔒	Shopping	p138

Sights

Botanic Gardens
PARK

1 ◉ MAP P126, C1

A marvellous thing about walking in here is the way the noise of Great Western Rd suddenly recedes into the background. The wooded gardens follow the riverbank of the River Kelvin and there are plenty of tropical species to discover. **Kibble Palace**, an impressive Victorian iron and glass structure dating from 1873, is one of the largest glasshouses in Britain; check out the herb garden, too, with its medicinal species. (☏0141-276 1614; www.glasgowbotanicgardens.com; 730 Great Western Rd; ☺7am-dusk, glasshouse 10am-6pm summer, to 4.15pm winter)

Kelvin Hall
MUSEUM

2 ◉ MAP P126, B4

Opened in the 1920s as an exhibition centre, this enormous sandstone palace, renovated and reopened in 2016, is a mixed leisure and arts space. As well as a gym and sports facilities, it hosts the audiovisual archive of the National Library of Scotland (p128) and also stores items from the University of Glasgow's museum collection (available by appointment). The major exhibition halls are being developed and may end up holding the Hunterian collections as well as other city-related exhibits. (☏0141-276 1450; www.

glasgowlife.org.uk; 1445 Argyle St; admission free; ☺6.30am-10pm Mon-Fri, 8am-5pm Sat, 8am-8pm Sun)

Kelvingrove Park
PARK

3 ◉ MAP P126, D5

On both banks of the meandering River Kelvin, a tributary of the Clyde, this West End park is popular with dog walkers, foot commuters and canoodling students from the nearby university. It hosted the 1888 and 1901 International Exhibitions; the latter saw the opening of the Kelvingrove Art Gallery & Museum (p116), the park's most notable structure.

Fossil Grove
NATURAL FEATURE

4 ◉ MAP P126, A4

In pretty Victoria Park, these dozen or so fossilised leptodendron stumps date from the Carboniferous period, some 320 million years ago, and are an intriguing sight. To get here, take bus 44 from the city centre. (☏0141-950 1448; www.glasgow.gov.uk; Victoria Park, Dumbarton Rd; admission free; ☺noon-4pm Sat & Sun Apr–mid-Oct)

National Library of Scotland
ARCHIVES

5 ◉ MAP P126, B5

In Kelvin Hall (p128), this outpost of Edinburgh's National Library of Scotland hosts a small exhibition and a digital archive of maps and audiovisual material. You can also browse the library's digital collection here. You'll need an appointment to access some of the archives. (📞0845 366 4600; www.nls.uk; Kelvin Hall, 1445 Argyle St; admission free; 🕙10am-5pm Tue & Thu-Sat, 1.30-8pm Wed)

Eating

78 Cafe Bar CAFE, VEGETARIAN $

6 ✗ MAP P126, D6

More a comfortable lounge than your typical veggie restaurant, this offers cosy couch seating and reassuringly solid wooden tables, as well as an inviting range of ales. The low-priced vegan food includes hearty stews and curries, and there's regular live music in a very welcoming atmosphere.

(📞0141-576 5018; www.the78cafebar.com; 10 Kelvinhaugh St; mains £5-9; 🕙food noon-9pm; 🛜📶)

Bay Tree CAFE $

7 ✗ MAP P126, F3

There are a good many good cafes along this section of Great Western Road, but the Bay Tree is still a solid choice. It has lots of vegan and vegetarian options, smiling staff, filling mains (mostly Middle Eastern and Greek), generous salads and a good range of hot drinks. It's famous for its all-day breakfasts. (📞0141-334 5898; www.thebaytreewestend.co.uk; 403 Great Western Rd; mains £7-16; 🕙11am-10pm Tue-Fri, from 10am Sat & Sun; 🛜📶)

Kibble Palace, Botanic Gardens

The Glasgow Boys

The great rivalry between Glasgow and Edinburgh has also played out in the art world. In the late 19th century a group of Glaswegian painters challenged the artistic establishment that was dominant in the capital. Up to this point, paintings were largely confined to historical scenes and sentimental visions of the Highlands. These painters – including James Guthrie, EA Hornel, George Henry and Joseph Crawhall – experimented with colour and themes of rural life, shocking Edinburgh's conservative artistic society. Many of them went to study in Paris studios, and brought back a much-needed breath of European air into the Scottish art scene.

In the same period, Charles Rennie Mackintosh and Margaret Macdonald were members of a broader arts and design movement that became known as the Glasgow School, developing the distinctive art-nouveau Glasgow Style.

The movement had an enormous influence on the Scottish art world, inspiring the next generation of Scottish painters – the Colourists. In Glasgow, their works can be seen in the **Kelvingrove** (p116) and **Hunterian** (p121) galleries.

Hanoi Bike Shop   VIETNAMESE $

8 ✕ MAP P126, B2

Tucked away just off Byres Rd, this upbeat spot offers creative takes on Vietnamese food, using fresh ingredients and home-made tofu. The various pho dishes are delicious. Lunchtime *banh mi* and rice paper roll specials are a good deal. (☏0141-334 7165; www.hanoibikeshop.co.uk; 8 Ruthven Lane; mains £6-11; ☉noon-11pm; ☎)

Stravaigin   SCOTTISH, FUSION $$

9 ✕ MAP P126, E3

Stravaigin is a serious foodie's delight, with a menu constantly pushing the boundaries of originality and offering creative culinary excellence. With a range of eating spaces across three levels, it's pleasingly casual and easygoing. The entry level also has a buzzing bar with a separate menu. Scottish classics like haggis take their place alongside a range of Asian-influenced dishes. It's all delicious. (☏0141-334 2665; www.stravaigin.co.uk; 28 Gibson St; bar dishes £6-12, restaurant mains £15-19; ☉food 11am-11pm; ☎)

Ox & Finch   FUSION $$

10 ✕ MAP P126, D6

This fashionable place could almost sum up the thriving modern Glasgow eating scene, with a faux-pub name, sleek but comfortable contemporary decor, tapas-sized dishes and an open kitchen. Grab a cosy booth and be prepared to have your tastebuds wowed with innovative, delicious creations aimed at sharing, drawing on French and Mediterreanean influences but focusing on quality Scottish produce. (📞0141-339 8627; www.oxandfinch. com; 920 Sauchiehall St; small plates £4-10; 🕐noon-10pm; 🛜🍴)

Mother India INDIAN $$

11 🍽 MAP P126, D6

Glasgow curry buffs forever debate the merits of the city's numerous excellent South Asian restaurants; Mother India features in every discussion. It's been a stalwart for years, and the quality and innovation on show are superb. The three dining areas are all attractive and it makes an effort for kids, with a separate menu. (📞0141-221 1663; www.motherindia.co.uk; 28 Westminster Tce, Sauchiehall St; mains £11-16; 🕐5.30-10.30pm Mon-Thu, noon-11pm Fri, 1-11pm Sat, 1-10pm Sun; 🛜🍴👶)

Alchemilla MEDITERRANEAN $$

12 🍽 MAP P126, D6

The number of quality eating options opening on the Finnieston strip is phenomenal, and this is a fine example. A casual open-kitchen eatery, it offers small, medium and large plates with an eastern Mediterranean feel. Interesting ingredients and intriguing textures are key to delicious dishes ideal for sharing. There are

Hanoi Bike Shop

Ox & Finch (p130)

lots of meat-free options and a list of hard-to-find natural wines. (📞0141-337 6060; www.thisisalchemilla.com; 1126 Argyle St; plates £5-14; ⏱food noon-10pm)

The Finnieston   SEAFOOD $$

13 🍴 MAP P126, D6

A flagship of this increasingly vibrant strip, this gastropub recalls the area's sailing heritage with a cosily romantic below-decks atmosphere and artfully placed nautical motifs. It's been well thought through, with excellent G&Ts (slurp one in the little courtyard) and cocktails accompanying a short menu of high-quality upmarket pub fare focusing on sustainable Scottish seafood. Its brunches are also

recommendable. (📞0141-222 2884; www.thefinniestonbar.com; 1125 Argyle St; mains £13-23; ⏱food 11am-10pm Mon-Sat, to 9pm Sun; 📶)

Left Bank   BISTRO $$

14 🍴 MAP P126, E3

Huge windows fronting the street reveal this outstanding eatery specialising in gastronomic delights and lazy afternoons. Lots of little spaces filled with couches and chunky tables make for intimacy. The wide-ranging menu is good for devising a shared meal of delightful creations using seasonal and local produce, with an eclectic variety of influences. Breakfasts and brunches are also highlights. (📞0141-339 5969; www.theleftbank.co.uk; 33 Gibson St; mains £9-16; ⏱9am-10pm Mon-Fri, from 10am Sat & Sun; 📶🖉👪)

Number 16   BISTRO $$

15 🍴 MAP P126, A4

Run with warmth, this cosy narrow space near the bottom of Byres Rd is a pleasing spot for a short menu of quality Scottish cuisine based around excellent ingredients. Innovative flavour pairings add interest but never feel pretentious and some dishes really hit heights. Wines by the glass aren't a strong point. (📞0141-339 2544; www.number16.co.uk; 16 Byres Rd; mains £14-18; ⏱noon-2.30pm & 5.30-9pm Mon-Sat, 1-2.30pm & 5.30-8.30pm Sun)

Six by Nico
GASTRONOMY $$

16 ⊗ MAP P126, D6

Chefs are creative types and get easily bored whisking up the same menu day after day. Nico has fixed that by presenting a themed degustation that lasts for six weeks. Sometimes it will be focused on a specific national cuisine, other times it's a more whimsical subject, like Disney or Childhood. Presentation and quality are impeccable. (☏0141-334 5661; www.sixbynico.co.uk; 1132 Argyle St; tasting menu around £30, wine flight £25; ⊙noon-10pm Tue-Sun)

Wudon
ASIAN $$

17 ⊗ MAP P126, E2

Tasty sushi, fried noodles and ramen soups among other Asian dishes in a clean, contemporary setting. It's a friendly spot with helpful service. (☏0141-357 3033; www.wudon-noodlebar.co.uk; 535 Great Western Rd; dishes £9-12; ⊙12.30-10.30pm Tue-Sat, to 10pm Sun; ☎)

Bothy
SCOTTISH $$

18 ⊗ MAP P126, B2

This fab West End player, boasting a combo of modern design and comfy retro furnishings, blows apart the myth that Scottish food is stodgy and uninteresting. The Bothy dishes offer traditional home-style fare with a modern twist. It's filling, but leave room for dessert. Smaller lunch plates are a good deal, and there's an attractive outdoor

Bothy

area. (📞 0845 166 6032; www.
bothyglasgow.co.uk; 11 Ruthven Lane;
mains £12-20; 🕐 food noon-10pm
Mon-Fri, from 10am Sat & Sun; 🛜)

Òran Mór Brasserie PUB FOOD $$

This temple to Scottish dining
and drinking is a superb venue in
an old church (see 26 🍺 Map p126, C1).
Giving new meaning to the word
'conversion', the brasserie pumps
out high-quality bar meals in a
dark, Mackintosh-inspired space.
The conservatory area off the
main bar does cheaper bar meals.
(📞 0141-357 6226; www.oran-mor.
co.uk; cnr Great Western & Byres Rds;
brasserie mains £15-20; 🕐 5-9pm
Tue & Wed, noon-10pm Thu-Sat, noon-
9pm Sun; 🛜)

Ubiquitous Chip SCOTTISH $$$

19 ❌ MAP P126, B2

The original champion of Scottish
produce, this is legendary for
its still-unparalleled cuisine and
lengthy wine list. Named to poke
fun at Scotland's culinary reputation, it offers a French touch but
resolutely Scottish ingredients,
carefully selected and following
sustainable principles. The elegant courtyard space offers some
of Glasgow's best dining, while,
above, the cheaper brasserie
(longer hours) offers exceptional
value for money. (📞 0141-334
5007; www.ubiquitouschip.co.uk;
12 Ashton Lane; 2-/3-course lunch
£20/24, mains £20-30, brasserie
mains £13-16; 🕐 restaurant noon-

2.30pm & 5-11pm Mon-Sat, 12.30-3pm
& 5-10pm Sun; 🛜)

Butchershop Bar & Grill STEAK $$$

20 ❌ MAP P126, C5

Offering several different cuts of
traceably sourced, properly aged
beef, this is one of the best spots
in Glasgow for a tasty, served-as-
you-want-it steak. It's a perfect
lunch venue after the Kelvingrove
Art Gallery & Museum. There are
seats out the front if the weather
happens to be fine. It also has a
little seafood on the menu and
decently mixed cocktails. (📞 0141-
339 2999; www.butchershopglasgow.
com; 1055 Sauchiehall St; steaks £19-
36; 🕐 noon-10pm Sun-Thu, to 1am Fri
& Sat; 🛜)

Cail Bruich SCOTTISH $$$

21 ❌ MAP P126, C1

In an elegant if rather
on-descript dining room, the
kitchen here turns out some
memorable modern Scottish fare.
The forage ethos brings
surprising, tangy, herbal flavours
to plates that are always
interesting but never pretentious.
Everything from the amuse-
bouche to the homemade bread
is top-notch; the degustation
menu (£55) with optional wine
flight (£40) combines the
best on offer. (📞 0141-334 6265;
www.cailbruich.co.uk; 725 Great
Western Rd; 2-/3-course lunch
£22/28, set menus £45-55;

Local Experiences 👍

Riverside Wandering the riverside path along the Kelvin is a beautiful stroll through the heart of the district. Stop off at **Inn Deep** (p135) for a pint along the way.

Laneways Off the main thoroughfares, several laneways are venues for restaurants, quirky shops and craft studios. Ruthven Lane off Byres Rd has all three, while **De Courcy's Arcade** (p140) is a treasure trove of small vendors.

Curry There's nothing Glaswegians like more for dinner than a good curry and the city is full of tiptop South Asian restaurants. There are several longstanding local favourites dotted around the West End, with **Mother India** (p131) especially appreciated.

Vintage shopping Great Western and Byres Rds are well stocked with vintage shops, beloved of local students. **Glasgow Vintage Company** (p138) is one of the best established.

🕓6-9pm Mon & Tue, noon-2pm & 6-9pm Wed-Sat, 1-7pm Sun; 🛜)

Gannet SCOTTISH $$$

22 🍴 MAP P126, D6

In vogue but most certainly not starchy, this jewel of the Finnieston strip offers a cosy wood-panelled ambience and gourmet food that excels at presentation and taste without venturing towards cutting-edge. The short, polished daily menu features quality produce sourced mostly from southern Scotland and the interesting wine list backs it up very well indeed. Solicitous, professional service is another plus point. (📞0141-204 2081; www.thegannetgla.com; 1155 Argyle St; mains £21-25; 🕓5-9.30pm Tue &

Wed, noon-2pm & 5-9.30pm Thu-Sat, 1-7.30pm Sun; 🛜)

Drinking

Inn Deep BAR

23 🍺 MAP P126, E2

Descend the stairs to find yourself in a fabulous spot on the banks of the Kelvin. It's glorious on a fine day (and Glaswegians set that bar pretty low) to grab a craft beer and spill out onto the riverside path in a happy throng. The vaulted interior spaces under the bridge are also characterful. (📞0141-357 1075; www.inndeep.com; 445 Great Western Rd; 🕓noon-midnight Mon-Sat, 12.30-11pm Sun)

Kelvingrove Café

BAR, CAFE

24 ⊙ MAP P126, D6

A beautiful wood floor, elegant fittings and chessboard tiling give this place a stylish cosiness that perfectly matches its list of cocktails and G&Ts. It manages to straddle a few genres: the feeling of a timeworn local is offset by solicitous table service, while the food is a little more upmarket than it seems. (☑0141-221 8988; www.kelvingrovecafe.com; 1161 Argyle St; ⊙8am-midnight Mon-Sat, from 9am Sun; ☜)

Brewdog Glasgow

PUB

25 ⊙ MAP P126, B5

Perfect for a pint after the Kelvingrove Art Gallery & Museum, this great spot offers the delicious range of artisanal beers from the brewery of the same name. Punk IPA is refreshingly hoppy, with other favourites, new releases and guest beers also to explore. Tasting flights mean you can try several, while burgers and dogs are on hand to soak it up. (☑0141-334 7175; www.brewdog. com; 1397 Argyle St; ⊙noon-midnight; ☜)

Òran Mór

BAR, CLUB

26 ⊙ MAP P126, C1

Now some may be uncomfortable with the thought of drinking in a church. But we say: the Lord giveth. This bar, restaurant, club and theatre venue is a likeable

and versatile spot with an attractive interior and a fine whisky selection to replace the holy water. The lunchtime A Play, a Pie and a Pint (p138; Mondays to Saturdays at 1pm) is an excellent feature. (☑0141-357 6200; www.oran-mor. co.uk; cnr Byres & Great Western Rds; ⊙9am-2am Mon-Wed, to 3am Thu-Sat, 10am-3am Sun; ☜)

Brel

BAR

27 ⊙ MAP P126, B2

Perhaps the best bar on Ashton Lane, this joint can seem tightly packed, but there's a conservatory for eating out the back so you can pretend you're sitting outside when it's raining. When you're lucky enough that the sun does peek through, there's an appealing tiered beer garden. Its got a huge range of Belgian beers, and also does mussels and langoustines among other tasty fare. (☑0141-342 4966; www.brelbar.com; 39 Ashton Lane; ⊙noon-midnight Sun-Thu, to 1am Fri & Sat; ☜)

Hillhead Bookclub

BAR

28 ⊙ MAP P126, C1

Atmosphere in spades is the call sign of this easygoing West End bar. An ornate wooden ceiling overlooks two levels of well-mixed cocktails, seriously cheap drinks, comfort food and numerous intriguing decorative touches. There's even a ping-pong table in a cage, if the mood strikes. (☑0141-576 1700; www.hillhead

bookclub.co.uk; 17 Vinicombe St;
⏰11am-midnight Mon-Fri, from 10am
Sat & Sun; 📶)

Jinty McGuinty's

PUB

29 📍 MAP P126, B2

Unlike many Irish pubs, there's
actually something rather
authentically Irish about this
place, which has an aged
wooden floor, unusual booth
seating, a literary hall of fame and
a beer garden alongside. There's
live music most nights. (📞0141-
339 0747; www.facebook.com/
JintyMcguintysIrishBar; 23 Ashton
Lane; ⏰11am-midnight Mon-Sat, from
12.30pm Sun; 📶)

Tchai Ovna

TEAHOUSE

30 📍 MAP P126, E3

This student favourite on a West
End backstreet near the River
Kelvin is a relaxed den that has
nearly a hundred different teas
and other infusions on offer. It
also does vegetarian and vegan
food. (📞0141-357 4524; www.tchai
ovna.com; 42 Otago Lane; ⏰11am-
11pm; 📶)

Innis & Gunn
Beer Kitchen

MICROBREWERY

31 📍 MAP P126, B2

Set across three levels, this outpost of an Edinburgh brewery
offers some 20 taps of quality
craft beer, some of which
is brewed here, and a few

West End Drinking

Kelvingrove Café

LOU ARMOR/SHUTTERSTOCK ©

Brel (p136)

streetside tables. Food is available but doesn't quite hit this area's high standards. (☏0141-334 6688; www.innisandgunn.com; 44 Ashton Lane; ⏱10am-midnight; 🛜)

Vodka Wodka BAR

32 🚇 MAP P126, B2

Every vodka drinker's dream, Vodka Wodka has more varieties of the stealthy poison than you could possibly conquer in one sitting. Its brushed-metal bar dishes out the liquid fire straight and in cocktails to students during the day and groups of mid-20s in the evening. There's pleasant outdoor seating too. (☏0141-341 0669; www.vodkawodka.co.uk; 31 Ashton Lane; ⏱noon-midnight)

Entertainment

Hug & Pint LIVE MUSIC

33 ⭐ MAP P126, G3

With bands almost daily in the downstairs space, this comfortable local is a great destination. It would be anyway for its excellent atmosphere, highly original Asian-influenced vegan food and colourful interior. (☏0141-331 1901; www. thehugandpint.com; 171 Great Western Rd; ⏱noon-midnight; 🛜)

A Play, a Pie & a Pint THEATRE

This lunchtime theatre session at Òran Mór (p136; see 26 ⊕ MAP P126, C1) is a Glasgow classic. (☏0141-357 6200; www.playpiepint.com; Òran Mór, cnr Byres & Great Western Rds; £10-14 incl pie & pint; ⏱1pm Mon-Sat)

Grosvenor Cinema CINEMA

34 ⭐ MAP P126, B2

This sweet cinema puts you in the heart of West End eating and nightlife for post-show debriefings. (☏0845 166 6002; www.grosvenorwestend.co.uk; Ashton Lane)

Shopping

Glasgow Vintage Company VINTAGE

35 🔒 MAP P126, E2

With a little more breathing room than some of Glasgow's other vintage shops, this one offers relaxed browsing. (☏0141-338

6633; www.facebook.com/theglas
gowvintagecompany; 453 Great
Western Rd; ⏰11am-6pm Mon-Sat, to
5pm Sun)

Roots, Fruits & Flowers

FOOD & DRINKS

36 🔒 MAP P126, E2

With three separate entrances,
this store combines a florist,
an excellent fruit and vegetable
vendor, plus a larger organic
produce shop and deli that
includes a good bakery cafe.
(📞0141-334 3530; www.roots
fruitsandflowers.com; 455 Great
Western Rd; ⏰7am-7.30pm Mon-Fri,
to 6.30pm Sat, 9am-6.30pm Sun)

George Mewes Cheese

FOOD

37 🔒 MAP P126, B3

This temple to cheese is simply a
must-visit for all fans of the crum-
bly, pungent or creamy in life. The
open counter means the aromas
alone will tempt you to buy, but
helpful and friendly staff are keen
to offer you samples of anything
you would like to try. (📞0141-334
5900; www.georgemewescheese.co.uk;
106 Byres Rd; ⏰9am-6pm Mon-Sat,
from 10am Sun)

Valhalla's Goat

DRINKS

38 🔒 MAP P126, E2

The selection of worldwide
beers here, mostly of the small-
producer variety, has to be seen
to be believed. It also has an

Grosvenor Cinema

KAY ROXBY/ALAMY STOCK PHOTO ©

interesting wine selection and some very tasty handmade chocs. (📞0141-337 3441; www.valhallasgoat.com; 449 Great Western Rd; ⏰11am-10pm Mon-Fri, from 10am Sat, noon-8pm Sun)

De Courcy's Arcade

SHOPPING CENTRE

39 🅐 MAP P126, C2

Down a West End lane, this sweet, bijou two-level arcade has a selection of tiny boutiques offering vintage clothing, art, homewares and more. Opening hours of individual shops can vary. (www.facebook.com/decourcysarcade; Cresswell Lane; ⏰10am-5.30pm Mon-Sat, noon-5pm Sun)

Caledonia Books

BOOKS

40 🅐 MAP P126, E2

This characterful spot is just what a second-hand bookshop should be, with a smell of dust and venerability and a wide range of intriguing volumes on the slightly chaotic shelves. (📞0141-334 9663; www.caledoniabooks.co.uk; 483 Great Western Rd; ⏰10.30am-6pm Mon-Sat)

Papyrus

GIFTS & SOUVENIRS

41 🅐 MAP P126, C1

This innovative and upbeat West End store is a fine place to browse presents for folks back home, with everything from jewellery to homewares on offer. (📞0141-334 6514; www.papyrusgifts.

Hidden Lane

KAY ROXBY/ALAMY STOCK PHOTO ©

co.uk; 374 Byres Rd; ⊙9am-6pm Mon-Sat, from 11am Sun)

Hidden Lane ARTS & CRAFTS

42 🔒 MAP P126, D6

Well concealed down a passageway off the Finnieston strip, these back alleys house a colourful mix of arty shops and studios well worth investigating. There's a tearoom, jewellery store, yoga centre and plenty more. (www.thehiddenlaneglasgow.com; 1103 Argyle St)

Pink Poodle CLOTHING

43 🔒 MAP P126, C2

A wide range of designer clothing for women is stocked at this handsome, colourful boutique, with lots of unique items in a variety of styles. Prices aren't particularly cheap, but it's always an interesting browse. (📞0141-357 2983; www.pinkpoodleboutique.co.uk; 5-21 Cresswell Lane; ⊙10am-5.30pm Mon-Sat, noon-5pm Sun)

City Centre Comics BOOKS

44 🔒 MAP P126, B2

Tucked away in the Ruthven Lane complex, this has a sound range

of back issues, both recent and from past decades. Though the shop looks small, there's a huge selection. (📞0141-457 6325; www.citycentrecomics.com; 37 Ruthven Lane; ⊙10am-5pm Tue-Sat, noon-4pm Sun)

Shearer Candles ARTS & CRAFTS

45 🔒 MAP P126, C1

This West End shop of a family firm in business for well over a century has an excellent selection of original artisanal candles that are perfect for gifts. (📞0141-357 1707; www.shearer-candles.com; 388 Byres Rd; ⊙10am-6pm Mon-Sat, 11am-5pm Sun)

Antiques & Interiors ANTIQUES

46 🔒 MAP P126, B2

Up the back of the quirky Ruthven Lane complex, this arcade has several shops specialising in antiques, design and retro items. (www.antiques-atlas.com; Ruthven Lane; ⊙11am-5.30pm Mon-Sat, noon-5pm Sun)

Survival Guide

University of Glasgow (p120) CAPPAPHOTO/SHUTTERSTOCK ©

Before You Go

Book Your Stay

o Glasgow has plenty of accommodation but can still fill up at weekends; booking ahead is essential then, as well as in high season (July and August).

o Most providers set prices according to demand. Rates shoot up at weekends and reach stratospheric levels, even at mediocre places, if there's a big-name concert on a Saturday.

o By the same token, you can get excellent deals on quieter nights out of season.

o The city centre can get very rowdy at weekends, and accommodation options fill up fast, mostly with groups who will probably roll home boisterously some time after 3am. If you prefer an earlier appointment with your bed, you'll be better off in a smaller, quieter lodging, somewhere that takes soundproofing seriously, or in the West End.

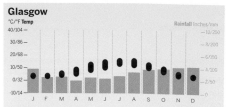

Glasgow

°C/°F Temp — Rainfall Inches/mm

When to Go

o Summer in Glasgow is a pleasure, with better weather and locals even cheerier than usual.

o Spring can also be lovely.

o Glasgow is super busy at weekends year-round; folk from elsewhere in Scotland head in to catch a show or go shopping.

Useful Websites

Lonely Planet (www.lonelyplanet.com/scotland/glasgow/hotels) Recommendations.

Visit Scotland (www.visitscotland.com/accommodation) Accommodation information and availability.

Best Budget

Glasgow SYHA (www.hostellingscotland.org.uk) Best budget option.

Heritage Hotel (www.theheritagehotel.net) Good-value West End hotel.

Euro Hostel (www.eurohostels.co.uk) Large, impersonal and central.

Best Midrange

Alamo Guest House (www.alamoguesthouse.com) Big range of excellent rooms in a top West End location.

Grasshoppers (www.grasshoppersglasgow.com) Excellent small, central hotel.

Amadeus Guest House (www.amadeusguesthouse.co.uk) Sunny B&B and great family apartments.

Z Hotel (www.thezhotels.com) Urban bolthole just off George Sq.

Pipers' Tryst Hotel (www.thepipingcentre.co.uk) Lovely spot attached to a bagpiping centre.

Best Top End

Dakota Deluxe (www.
dakotahotels.co.uk)
Eye-catching design
and seductive comfort.

15Glasgow (www.15
glasgow.com) Stunning
rooms at this boutique
B&B.

Blythswood Square
(www.blythswoods
quare.com) Georgian
architecture meets
modern elegance.

Malmaison (www.
malmaison.com) Sleek
and stylish hedonists'
choice.

Hotel du Vin (www.
hotelduvin.com) Opu-
lent West End retreat.

Arriving in Glasgow

Glasgow is easily
reached by air from
many British and
some European des-
tinations. It's about
an hour's flight from
London.

Trains and buses
reach the city from
London, Edinburgh
and numerous other
British cities.

Flights, cars and
tours can be booked
online at lonelyplanet.
com/bookings.

Glasgow International Airport

Ten miles west of the
city in Paisley, **Glasgow
International Airport**
(GLA; ☎ 0344 481 5555;
www.glasgowairport.com;
🛜) handles interna-
tional and domestic
flights. Facilities
include car hire, ATMs
and a supermarket
where you can buy SIM
cards.

Bus 500 runs every
10 or 15 minutes (half-
hourly or hourly late at
night) from Glasgow
International Airport to
Buchanan bus station
via Central and Queen
Street train stations
(single/return £8/12,
25 minutes). This is
a 24-hour service.
You can include a
day ticket on the bus
network for £12 total
or a four-day ticket
for £18.

Another bus, the 77,
covers the same route
via the West End twice
hourly, taking longer.

Taking a taxi costs
about £25.

Glasgow Prestwick Airport

Thirty miles southwest
of Glasgow near Ayr,
**Glasgoe Prestwick
Airport** (PIK; ☎ 0871 223
0700; www.glasgowprest-
wick.com) is used by Ry-
anair and some other
budget airlines, with
connections mostly to
southern Europe.

There's a dedi-
cated train station
at the airport, with
four trains an hour
(two on Sundays) to
Glasgow (£8.30, 40 to
55 minutes). You get
a 50% discount from
the airport by showing
your boarding pass.

At night, bus X99
replaces the train.

A taxi to the centre
of Glasgow costs £55
to £65.

Edinburgh Airport

There are direct buses
from the airport to
Glasgow (one hour).

Train

As a general rule,
**Glasgow Central
station** (www.scotrail.
co.uk; Gordon St) serves
southern Scotland,
England and Wales, and

Queen Street station

(www.scotrail.co.uk; George St) serves the north and east (including Edinburgh). Buses run between the two stations every 10 minutes. There are direct trains more than hourly to London Euston station; they're much quicker (4½ hours) and more comfortable than the bus. The fare is £65/142/183 for advance/off-peak/anytime singles.

ScotRail (☑ 0344 811 0141; www.scotrail.co.uk) runs Scottish trains. Destinations include the following:

Aberdeen (£41.80, 2½ to 3½ hours, hourly)

Dundee (£23.20, 1½ hours, hourly)

Edinburgh (£14.40, 50 minutes, every 15 minutes)

Fort William (£30.80, 3¾ hours, four daily)

Inverness (£92.50; 3½ to four hours; five direct daily, three on Sunday)

Oban (£25.30, three hours, three to six daily)

Buchanan Street Bus Station

All long-distance buses arrive at and depart from **Buchanan bus station** (☑ 0141-333 3708; www.spt.co.uk; Killermont St; ☏), which has pricey lockers, ATMs and wi-fi.

Megabus (☑ 0141-352 4444; www.megabus.com) Your first port of call if you're looking for the cheapest fare. Megabus offers very cheap demand-dependent prices on many major bus routes, including to Edinburgh and London.

National Express (☑ 0871 781 8181; www.nationalexpress.com) Runs daily to several English cities.

Scottish Citylink (☑ 0871 266 3333; www.citylink.co.uk) Has buses to Edinburgh (£7.90, 1¼ hours, every 15 minutes) and most major towns in Scotland.

There are also buses from Buchanan bus station direct to/from Edinburgh Airport (£12, one hour, half-hourly).

Car & Motorcycle

Glasgow is about 400 miles north of London; think about an eight-hour drive. The M8 connects Edinburgh and Glasgow; approximately an hour's drive depending on traffic.

Greenock Cruise Port

Regular trains run from Greenock to Glasgow (35 to 50 minutes).

Getting Around

Bus

○ City bus services, mostly run by **First Glasgow** (☑ 0141-420 7600; www.firstglasgow.com), are frequent.

○ You can buy tickets when you board buses, but on most you must have the exact change.

○ Short journeys in town cost £1.60 or £2.30; a day ticket (£4.50) is good value and is valid until 1am, when a night network starts. A weekly ticket is £17.

○ Check route maps online at www.spt.co.uk.

Subway

○ The circular underground line, the Subway, serves 15 stations in the city centre, and west and south of the city (single £1.70).

o The train network connects with the subway at Buchanan Street underground station, next to **Queen Street overground station** (www.scotrail.co.uk; George St), and St Enoch underground station, near **Glasgow Central station** (www.scotrail. co.uk; Gordon St).

o The All Day Ticket (£4.10) gives unlimited travel on the subway for a day, while the Roundabout ticket gives a day's unlimited train and subway travel for £7.

o The subway runs roughly from 6.30am to 11.30pm Monday to Saturday but annoyingly runs only from 10am to 6pm on Sunday.

Taxi

o There's no shortage of taxis, and if you want to know anything about Glasgow, striking up a conversation with a cabbie is a good place to start.

o Fares are very reasonable – you can get across the city centre for around £6, and there's no surcharge for calling a taxi.

o You can pay by credit card with **Glasgow Taxis** (☑0141-429 7070; www.glasgowtaxis.co.uk) if you order by phone; most of its taxis are wheelchair accessible. Download its app to make booking easy.

Train

o There's an extensive suburban network of trains in and around Glasgow; tickets should be purchased before travel if the departing station is staffed, or from the conductor if it isn't.

Car & Motorcycle

o The most difficult thing about driving in Glasgow is the sometimes-confusing one-way system.

o For short-term parking (up to two hours), you've got a decent chance of finding something on the street and paying at the meters, which cost up to £4 per hour. Otherwise, multistorey car parks are probably your best bet and are not prohibitively expensive.

Daytripper Tickets

The Daytripper ticket gives you a day's unlimited travel on buses, the subway, rail and some ferries in the Glasgow region, including Loch Lomond, Ayrshire and Lanarkshire. It costs £12.30 for one adult or £21.80 for two. Two kids per adult are included free.

o Ask your hotel in advance if it offers parking discounts.

o There are numerous car-rental companies; you will find that both big names and discount operators have airport offices.

Arnold Clark (☑0141-423 9559; www.arnold-clarkrental.com; 43 Allison St; ☺8am-5.30pm Mon-Fri, to 4pm Sat, 11am-4pm Sun)

Avis (☑0344 544 6064; www.avis.co.uk; 70 Lancefield St; ☺8am-6pm Mon-Fri, to 3pm Sat, 10am-2pm Sun)

Enterprise (☑ 0141-221 2124; www.enterprise. co.uk; 40 Oswald St; ⊙7am-9pm Mon-Fri, 8am-4pm Sat, 10am-3pm Sun)

Europcar (☑ 0371 384 3471; www.europcar. co.uk; 76 Lancefield Quay; ⊙8am-6pm Mon-Fri, to 4pm Sat)

Hertz (☑ 0141-229 6120; www.hertz.co.uk; Jury's Inn, 80 Jamaica St; ⊙8am-6pm Mon-Fri, to 1pm Sat, 10am-2pm Sun)

Bicycle

The **Nextbike** (www.next bike.co.uk; per 30min £1) citybike scheme is easy; download the app for the most convenient use.

There are also several places to hire a bike; check in at the **tourist office** (p151) for a full list.

Gear Bikes (☑ 0141-339 1179; www.gearbikes. com; 19 Gibson St; half-day/day/week £15/20/80; ⊙10am-6pm Mon-Sat, noon-5pm Sun)

Bike for Good (☑ 0141-248 5409; www. bikeforgood.org.uk; 65 Haugh Rd; half-day/day/week £15/20/70; ⊙9am-5pm Mon-Sat, to 8pm Wed)

Essential Information

Accessible Travel

o Download Lonely Planet's free Accessible Travel guides from https://shop.lonely planet.com/categories/accessible-travel

o Most new buildings are accessible to wheelchair users, so modern hotels and tourist attractions are fine. However, most B&Bs and guesthouses are in hard-to-adapt older buildings, which means that travellers with mobility problems may pay more for accommodation.

o Newer buses have steps that lower for easier access, as do trains, but it's wise to check before setting out. Tourist attractions usually reserve parking spaces near the entrance for drivers with disabilities.

o Many places such as ticket offices and banks are fitted with hearing loops to assist the hearing-impaired; look for a posted symbol of a large ear.

o An increasing number of tourist attractions have audio guides. Some have Braille guides or scented gardens for the visually impaired.

o VisitScotland produces the guide *Accessible Scotland* for wheelchair-using travellers. Its website (www.visitscotland. com) details accessible accommodation.

o DisabledGo (www. disabledgo.com) provides audited information on specific sites and venues in Glasgow.

Business Hours

Typical opening hours:

Banks 9.30am–4pm or 5pm Monday to Friday; some open 9.30am–1pm Saturday

Nightclubs 9pm or 10pm–1am, 2am or later; often only open Thursday to Saturday

Post offices 9am–6pm Monday to Friday, 9am–12.30pm Saturday (main branches to 5pm Saturday)

Pubs & bars 11am–11pm Monday to Thursday, 11am–1am Friday and Saturday, noon–11pm Sunday

Restaurants Lunch

noon–2.30pm, dinner
6pm–9pm

Shops 9am–6pm Monday to Saturday, often
11am–5pm Sunday

COVID-19

○ Glasgow had some of
the UK's strictest
COVID-19 lockdown
rules during 2020 and
2021. It is worth checking current requirements ahead of a visit.

○ Requirements for
travel to Scotland can be
found at https://www.
gov.scot/publications/
coronavirus-covid-
19-international-travel-
quarantine/

○ Details of current rules
and facilities in Glasgow
are at https://www.glas
gow.gov.uk/coronavirus

Discount Cards

There are no really
worthwhile discount
cards specific to Glasgow, but membership
of the **National Trust
for Scotland** (☑ 0131-
458 0200; www.nts.org.
uk; annual membership
adult/family £57/102) and
Historic Environment Scotland (HES;
☑ 0131-668 8999; www.
historicenvironment.scot;
annual membership adult/

family £55/101) is worth
considering if you
are travelling further
around the country.

Electricity

Type G
230V/50Hz

Emergency & Important Numbers

UK country code	☑ 44
International access code	☑ 00
All emergencies	☑ 999
Police (non-emergency)	☑ 101

Hospitals

Glasgow Dental Hospital (☑ 0141-211
9600; www.nhsggc.org.uk;
378 Sauchiehall St)

Glasgow Royal Infirmary (☑ 0141-211
4000; www.nhsggc.org.
uk; 84 Castle St) Medical
emergencies and out-
patient facilities.

Queen Elizabeth University Hospital
(☑ 0141-201 1100; www.
nhsggc.org.uk; 1345 Govan
Rd) Modern; south of
the river.

Internet Access

There's a free wi-fi
zone across the city
centre. You can get
a local SIM card for
about a pound and
data packages are
cheap.

Gallery of Modern Art
(☑ 0141-229 1996; www.
glasgowlife.org.uk; Royal
Exchange Sq; ☉10am-5pm
Mon-Wed & Sat, to 8pm Thu,
11am-5pm Fri & Sun; ☎)
Basement library; free
internet access. Book-
ings recommended.

Hillhead Library
(☑ 0141-276 1617; www.
glasgowlife.org.uk; 348
Byres Rd; ☉10am-8pm
Mon-Thu, to 5pm Fri & Sat,
noon-5pm Sun; ☎) Free
internet terminals.

iCafe (☑ 0141-353 6469;
www.icafe.uk.com; 250
Woodlands Rd; per hr £2.50;
☉8.30am-9.30pm; ☎)
Sip a coffee and munch

Dos and Don'ts

Greetings Shake hands when meeting for the first time. Female friends are greeted with a single kiss.

Football Be aware of the strength of feelings of local supporters before discussing the latest Old Firm match.

Pub culture Locals drink in rounds; one person buys the drinks for everyone, then it's the next person's turn. Order at the bar; food will usually be brought to your table when ready.

Transport Let people off before boarding yourself.

on a pastry while you check your emails on super-fast connections. Wi-fi too. It's actually a very good cafe in its own right. There are other branches, including one on **Sauchiehall St** (0141-353 1553; www.icafe.uk.com; 315 Sauchiehall St; 7am-10pm Mon-Fri, from 8am Sat & Sun;).

Mitchell Library (0141-287 2999; www.glasgowlife.org.uk; North St; 9am-8pm Mon-Thu, to 5pm Fri & Sat) Free internet access; bookings recommended.

Yeeha Internet Cafe (www.yeeha-internet-cafe.co.uk; 2nd fl, 48 West George St; per hr £2.50; 9.30am-6pm Mon-Fri, from 10am Sat) Upstairs

location in the heart of the city.

Money

ATMs (cashpoints) widely available. Credit cards are accepted in most (but not all) places, sometimes with a minimum spend or surcharge.

Tipping

Hotels One pound per bag is standard; tips for cleaning staff optional.

Pubs Not expected.

Restaurants For decent service tip 10%, and up to 15% at more expensive places.

Taxis Round up to nearest pound.

Public Holidays

Although bank holidays are general public holidays in the rest of the UK, in Scotland they only apply to banks and some other commercial offices.

General public holidays:

New Year 1 and 2 January

Good Friday March or April

Easter Monday March or April

May Day First Monday in May

Spring Holiday Last Monday in May

Glasgow Fair Saturday before the 3rd Monday in July

Autumn Holiday Last Monday in September

Christmas Day 25 December

Boxing Day 26 December

Responsible Travel

Glasgow isn't over-touristed and so there are no specific places where sensitivity is required on that front. However, the principles of responsible and sustainable travel are important:

o Try to buy from local providers rather than national or international chains

o Prioritise those businesses who make an effort to be sustainable

o Walk, cycle or use public transport

o Use official accommodation providers rather than unlicensed apartment rentals as these can drive rents up for locals.

Safe Travel

Glasgow is a safe city and you're unlikely to have any problems if you follow normal big-city precautions.

o Nightlife at weekends can get very boisterous.

o The football rivalry between Rangers and Celtic is a serious one; don't get involved in banter unless you under stand the context.

Telephone

o Roaming charges within the EU have been eliminated (though charges

may reappear when the UK leaves the EU).

o Other international roaming charges can be prohibitively high, and you'll probably find it cheaper to get a UK number. This is easily done by buying a SIM card (around £1) and sticking it in your phone. Your phone may be locked to your home network, however, so you'll have to either get it unlocked, or buy a cheap phone to use.

o Operators offer a variety of packages that include UK calls, messages and data; a month's worth will typically cost around £20. Recharges can be done online or by buying vouchers from shops.

Phone Codes

Dialling the UK Dial your country's international access code then ☏44 (the UK country code), then the area code (dropping the first '0') followed by the telephone number.

Dialling out of the UK The international access code is ☏00; dial this,

then add the code of the country you wish to dial.

Area code Glasgow's area code is 0141. Drop the zero if dialling from abroad.

Free calls Numbers starting with ☏0800 are free; calls to ☏0345 and ☏0845 numbers are charged at local rates.

Toilets

The council website www.glasgow.gov. uk has a list and a map of public toilets in Glasgow. Most are free; some have a small charge.

Tourist Information

Glasgow Tourist Office (www.visitscotland. com; 158 Buchanan St; ⊙9am-5pm Mon-Sat, 10am-4pm Sun Nov-Apr, 9am-6pm Mon-Sat, 10am-4pm Sun May, Jun, Sep & Oct, 9am-7pm Mon-Sat, 10am-5pm Sun Jul & Aug; ☎) The city's tourist office is in the centre of town. It opens at 9.30am on Thursday mornings.

Behind the Scenes

Send Us Your Feedback

We love to hear from travellers – your comments help make our books better. We read every word, and we guarantee that your feedback goes straight to the authors. Visit **lonelyplanet.com/contact** to submit your updates and suggestions.

Note: We may edit, reproduce and incorporate your comments in Lonely Planet products such as guidebooks, websites and digital products, so let us know if you are happy to have your name acknowledged. For a copy of our privacy policy visit lonelyplanet.com/legal.

Andy's Thanks

It's always a huge pleasure to enjoy the very generous hospitality of Jenny Neil and Brendan Bolland, and to work with Neil Wilson, Cliff Wilkinson and the excellent LP team. Numerous other people have been very generous with time and information. I'd particularly like to thank Robin Mitchell, Maggie Maguire, Graeme Campbell, Jen Stewart and the staff at many tourist information offices.

Acknowledgements

Cover photograph: Glasgow Science Centre, IMAX and Glasgow Tower: Binson Calfort/Shutterstock ©

Back cover photograph: Argyll Arcade, Buchanan Street; Treasure-Galore/Shutterstock ©

Photographs pp32-3 (clockwise from top left): lou armor; Jeff Whyte; EQRoy ©

This Book

This second edition of Lonely Planet's *Pocket Glasgow* guidebook was researched and written by Andy Symington. This guidebook was produced by the following:

Destination Editors
James Smart, Clifton Wilkinson

Senior Product Editors
Angela Tinson, Genna Patterson

Cartographer
Mark Griffiths

Product Editors
Sarah Farrell, Joel Cotterell

Book Designers
Gwen Cotter, Clara Monitto

Assisting Editors
Sarah Bailey, Michelle Bennett, Nigel Chin, Kellie Langdon, Kate Mathews, Kristin Odijk

Cover Researcher
Gwen Cotter

Thanks to Ronan Abayawickrema, Heather Champion, Fergal Condon, Katie Connolly, Karen Henderson, Sonia Kapoor, Anne Mason, Darren O'Connell, Martine Power, Lyahna Spencer

Index

See also separate subindexes for:

⊗ **Eating p155**

☺ **Drinking p155**

✪ **Entertainment p156**

🄰 **Shopping p156**

Our Writer

Andy Symington

Andy has written or worked on more than 100 books and other updates for Lonely Planet (especially in Europe and Latin America) and other publishing companies, and has published articles on numerous subjects for a variety of newspapers, magazines, and websites. He part-owns and operates a rock bar, has written a novel and is currently working on several fiction and non-fiction writing projects. When he's not off with a backpack in some far-flung corner of the world, he can probably be found watching the tragically poor local football side or tasting local wines after a long walk in the nearby mountains.

Published by Lonely Planet Global Limited
CRN 554153
2nd edition – Jul 2022
ISBN 978 1 78868 096 7
© Lonely Planet 2022   Photographs © as indicated 2022
10 9 8 7 6 5 4 3 2 1
Printed in Malaysia

Although the authors and Lonely Planet have taken all reasonable care in preparing this book, we make no warranty about the accuracy or completeness of its content and, to the maximum extent permitted, disclaim all liability arising from its use.